BRASIL TERRA VIRGEM

TERRA VIRGEM
EDITORA

Publishers
Ana Augusta Rocha, Roberto Linsker

Texts
Ana Augusta Rocha

Photography
Aristides Alves, Ed Viggiani, Felipe Goifman, José Leopoldo Plentz,
Leonide Principe, Loren McIntyre, Miguel Aun, Pedro Martinelli,
Roberto Linsker, Rui Faquini, Valdemir Cunha, Zig Koch.

History Consultant
Ana Ligabue

Image Editing
Roberto Linsker

Design and Art Direction
Cláudio Novaes/**BRAND**group

Art Finishing
Maria del Mar Reyes

Graphic Production
Márcia Signorini

English Version
Peter Musson

Editorial Coordination
Roberto Linsker

Legal Advice
José Paulo Brito

Administration
Nelson M. de Souza Jr.

Secretary
Maria Sílvia de Abreu Souza

CTP and Printed by
Graficos Burti

TERRA VIRGEM EDITORA - Rua Galeno de Almeida, 179 - São Paulo - SP - 05410-030 - Brasil
Tel./Fax 11 3081-9932/3083-7823 - e-mail: terravirgem@terravirgem.com.br

BRASIL
TERRA
VIRGEM

COORDINATION: ANA AUGUSTA ROCHA AND ROBERTO LINSKER

TERRA VIRGEM
EDITORA

Ilustrations: Alex Cerveny

CONTENTS

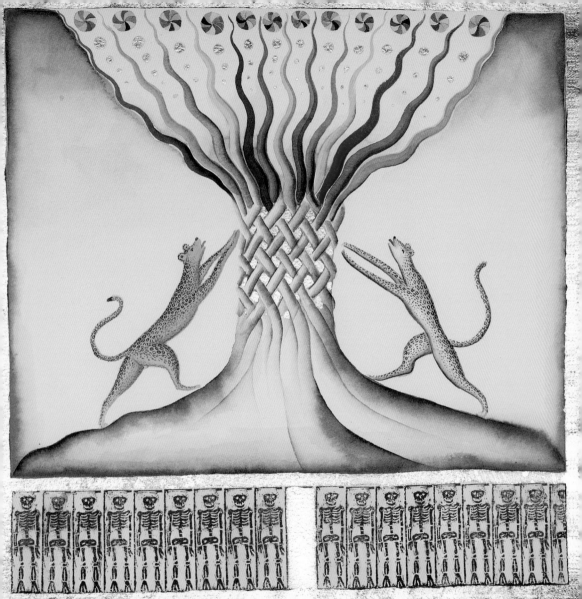

The word virgin,

in its most original form,
meant that which
belongs to no one, that which
belongs to itself alone:
an allusion to integrity and
entireness.

Brasil Terra Virgem

is more than a title,
more than the name
of a publishing house: it is our desire
for Brazil.

That which is not integral
is disintegrated.

COLLABORATORS

Leonide Principe

Photographing Brazil, especially the Amazon, has allowed me to see at first hand the vast biological heritage of this land, green par excellence. Daily contact with the unique nature found here, the discovery of its vegetable and animal species, its inhabitants and their customs has something special that touches the sphere of sentiment. In my experience of Brazil, or rather the Amazon, this sentiment is intrinsic to my work, and is above all an opportunity to gain knowledge and living experience at first hand.

Felipe Golfman

I have been photographing Brazil for more than a decade, directing my work at the line that separates documentation and esthetics. It is in the explosion of colors of Brazilian ecosystems, where the elements essential to man's adaptation to the environment are found, that I find my greatest inspiration. My delight is being in contact with the formation of Brazilian culture as it happens and taking photographs that are able to tell stories of the mixture of peoples that is Brazil.

Miguel Aun

To photograph Brazil is to try and document an almost endless universe: more than eight million square kilometers, infinitely varied human and geographical landscapes, colors of every tone and nuance, gestures and customs that have the power to reveal that which is unsuspected at first sight. For some time now I have been travelling around a piece of this photogenic country, principally the trails of Minas Gerais, from the open plateaus to the interiors and back yards of our small towns. What fascinates me most is the people living there. I'm filled with admiration for the forms of their buildings, the harmony of colors, the unexpected movement of their daily rhythms. This is the great adventure: to capture the beauty underneath the simple exterior.

Zig Koch

Photographing Brazil signifies becoming ever more Brazilian and having the privilege to understand this country of ours a little better. It also means having the opportunity to show images of the real face of Brazil to an ever-larger number of Brazilians. My hope is therefore that people will learn to admire our country, to love and preserve it so that future generations will have the chance to know it as it is – in all its essence and splendor – one of the most beautiful countries in the world.

Pedro Martinelli

Brazil is a country where diversity has reached its peak. It must be discovered on every corner, for each one has its own history, identity, its way of life. That is, Brazil is not just a country, it is a mosaic formed of thousands of pieces, each one unique. Before speaking of or revealing this vast country, one must look at it with humility: much humility. To seek out, look up close, converse, understand, and above all, learn from the local people. They hold the knowledge that we all need in order to maintain intact our riches – whether human, natural or cultural. Legislation alone is not enough. One has to go out and see and listen...

Aristides Alves

The light in the first hours of day and at afternoon's end reveals the most beautiful spectacles of color and form. The light radiated by the people brings joy and seduces us with its emotion. Light, people, nature, architecture, tones, brilliance, rhythm, composition. All this, and much more, makes Brazil's Northeast the most interesting region to photograph and experience.

Rui Faquini

To photograph Brazil is to be totally transformed by the challenge, so great and full of contrast is it that the photographer is converted to a kind of religion of freedom, to be endlessly reborn.

Loren McIntyre

When I come to Brazil to photograph, I am welcomed into societies of an astonishing range from hunter-gatherers in the forest to friends who dine in tall buildings. When I go away, I miss them all.

Leopoldo Plentz

Photographing Brazil is a challenge due to its continental size, and also its cultural diversity, demanding of the photographer knowledge of much more than just photography.

Valdemir Cunha

The desire to get to know and divulge through my images a Brazil that is still unknown to most people is what drives me, whenever I can, to pack my bags and take to the road, our roads.

Ed Viggiani

Photographing Brazil is an attempt at understanding different accents with the eye. It is a search to find the image that defines our identity.

THIS BOOK CAN BE LIKENED TO A TREE, THE BRAZILIAN TREE, IMAGINED AND IMAGINARY, WHICH PROTECTS US, COVERS US, AND RAISES US ON ITS BRANCHES TOWARD THE SKY, TOWARD THE LIGHT SO THAT THE SUCCESSES AND FAILURES OF LIFE CAN BE INSCRIBED ON ITS ILLUMINATED LEAVES.

LIKE ALL TREES, IT BEGAN ITS LIFE AS A SEED THAT GERMINATED AND GREW ON FERTILE SOIL. DAY AFTER DAY, YEAR AFTER YEAR, THE LEAVES SUCCEEDED ONE ANOTHER AFTER EACH RAINFALL, EACH JOURNEY, WITHOUT INTERRUPTION.

FOR TIME DOES NOT WAIT. THE SAME TIME THAT CANNOT BE WON BACK, AND THEREFORE, MUCH LESS LOST.

POETS HAVE TOLD US: "THERE ARE NO PATHS MARKED FOR THE TRAVELER, THE WAY IS MADE CLEAR AS ONE TRAVELS". BY TRAVELING THESE PATHS WE ENCOUNTER SILENCE, MURMURS, MUSIC AND VOICES. VOICES RECOUNTING STORIES, AT THE ROADSIDE OR AT JOURNEY'S END, SHOOTING THE BREEZE IN A BAR OR IN A NEIGHBORLY HOUSE IN THE DISTANT BACKLANDS. WE DISCOVER AS WE LISTEN THE BRAZIL WHICH IS MOST IN TOUCH WITH ITSELF, WHICH BLOOMS AS A GENUINE REFLECTION OF THOSE WHO LIVE ROOTED IN THEIR LAND AND UNDERSTAND THE LANDSCAPE SURROUNDING THEM.

WE LISTEN AND WE WATCH SO AS NOT TO BE RESTRICTED TO IMAGINATION.

THAT WHICH I SEE CROSSING THE SKIES, THE SEAS, IN MY STEPS: IMAGES CUT OUT FROM TIME AND KEPT ALIVE IN MEMORY; IMAGES OF A BRAZIL THAT CHANGES SO QUICKLY, GOING FROM THE UNHEARD-OF TO THE INTIMATE IN A MATTER OF MOMENTS: TELEVISION MOMENTS.

THE IDEA IS NOT, WAS NOT NOR EVER WILL BE, TO CAPTURE ONLY THE REMOTE UNKNOWN, THE SOURCE OF CURIOSITY AND SURPRISES, BUT THAT WHICH DESERVES OUR UNDERSTANDING, WHICH NEEDS LIGHT AND ALSO SHADE. WE SIT, THEREFORE, UNDER THE TREE.

R. LINSKER

IN 1994 I SET OUT ON THE ROAD TO DISCOVER BRAZIL AND HAVE NOT STOPPED YET.

THAT DATE MARKED THE BEGINNING OF THE BRASIL AVENTURA SERIES AND SINCE THEN WE HAVE PUBLISHED ONE BOOK PER YEAR; THE 1999 EDITION BEING THE LAST IN THIS FORMAT AND PERIODICITY.

I NEVER COULD HAVE IMAGINED, AT THE BEGINNING, THAT THIS ROAD THAT HAS TAKEN ME TO SO MANY PLACES OVER THE LAST SIX YEARS WOULD ALSO LEAD ME ON AN INTERNAL JOURNEY IN SUCH A VISCERAL MANNER THAT, EVERY TIME I SIT DOWN TO WRITE, SOME STORY SPRINGS UP TELLING US SOMETHING OF OUR COUNTRY.

AS IF OUR RIVERS WERE MY OWN VEINS, OUR LAND MY OWN FLESH, AND THE EXPRESSION HERE AND NOW A POSSIBILITY.

MY GREATEST FEAR IS THAT THE CHANGES ARE OCCURRING TOO FAST, AND THAT IN THE WHIRLWIND OF GLOBALIZATION, CONCESSIONS AND "PROGRESS", WE WILL LOSE A PRECIOUS PART OF OUR IDENTITY.

FOR THIS REASON, BOOKS MAKE A BEAUTIFUL AND ALMOST PERENNIAL REMINDER.

IT IS MY HOPE THAT THIS SERIES EXPRESSES AT LEAST A SMALL PART OF THE IMMENSE BEAUTY OF OUR LAND AND ITS PEOPLE.

ANA AUGUSTA ROCHA

ROOTS

TO THE CHILDREN OF THE EARTH,
KNOW THE SOIL FROM WHICH WE OBTAIN OUR ESSENCE.

* Ricardo Guimarães works in advertising at Guimarães Profissionais, SP.

You have to be courageous and dig deep to find our roots.

Courage for sure, for together with the spade that brings up the soil we bring to light some corpses, for not even the passage of one hundred, two hundred or five hundred years can erase the rottenness of the past.

One also has to dig deep into the immensity of the Brazilian tree: stretching for the same extent and with the same grandeur of the canopy – our branches and boughs extending over half a continent – are the long roots underground. Courage, as the inspired Ricardo Guimarães* said, is to act with the heart

INDIANS

PORTUGUESE

AFRICANS

(from the French Coeur + Agir) and it is with this that we will do our archeology.

As we dig we disinter a nightmare called slavery; we will disinter the infinite sadness of – as a nation – having annihilated six hundred indigenous peoples.

But at the same time, despite all

that has disappeared, an enormous faith will be found to flourish: faith in life, work with faith, faith in luck, that better times are around the corner, that our team will win and that, at the end, everything will work out all right.

Work out right in the sense of being true, whole, even if plural.

Although soiled with earth, gasping for breath, we see at last that the fine porcelain shards of the masters' dinner services, the pieces of the earthenware bowls of the slave quarters and the slivers of tribal stone tools emerge inseparably from the earth: the amalgamated fragments of our soul.

Left page: Peruaçu-MG ©R. Linsker / Still photo ©Gui von Schmidt

PINDORAMA

AMERINDIAN ROOTS.

SÃO PAULO ARCHEOLOGIST NIÉDE GUIDON HAS A THEORY THAT AMERICANS HOTLY CONTEST: THAT THE FIRST INHABITANTS OF THE AMERICAS ARRIVED FIRST IN BRAZIL AROUND 45,000 YEARS AGO, BY SEA, AND NOT FROM NORTH AMERICA VIA THE BERING LAND BRIDGE. THIS POSSIBLE FIRST LANDFALL FOR OUR INDIANS DOES NOT, HOWEVER, SIGNIFY A GREAT VICTORY: IT ONLY INDICATES INCREASED KNOWLEDGE OF A HISTORY IGNORED AND UNKNOWN FOR CENTURIES.

THE FIRST OF MANY INSTANCES OF IGNORANCE ORIGINATED WITH THE GENOVESE SAILOR CHRISTOPHER COLOUMBUS: IN 1492, UPON MAKING LAND ON ISLANDS NEAR THE PRESENT VENEZUELAN COAST, HE THOUGHT HE HAD REACHED INDIA, AND THEREFORE CALLED THE INDIGENOUS INHABITANTS INDIANS. THE CONTINUED USE OF THIS SINGLE TERM TO DESIGNATE SUCH NUMEROUS AND DIVERSE PEOPLES REVEALS THE ENORMOUS IGNORANCE WE HAVE ALWAYS SHOWN ABOUT THEM.

WE KNOW ONLY THAT IN 1500 THEY WERE MANY, CERTAINLY FAR MORE NUMEROUS THAN THE INHABITANTS OF PORTUGAL, WHICH AT THE TIME HAD A POPULATION OF NO MORE THAN ONE MILLION ONE HUNDRED THOUSAND. IT IS ESTIMATED THAT IN BRAZIL THERE WERE FROM FIVE TO TEN MILLION INHABITANTS BELONGING TO MORE THAN ONE THOUSAND ETHNIC GROUPS, WITH HUNDREDS OF SEPARATE LANGUAGES.

THE LETTER AND ITS MESSAGE.

PERO VAZ DE CAMINHA, NARRATOR OF THE FIRST MEETING OF CABRAL'S SQUADRON WITH THE COASTAL TUPIS, CLASSIFIED THEM AS HANDSOME AND INNOCENT. HE DESCRIBED BRAZIL AS A PARADISE OF COLORED BIRDS, EXUBERANT VEGETATION AND – HE ADDED WITH GREAT CONVICTION. INHABITED BY A PEOPLE THAT COULD BE EASILY ADAPTED.

"THEIR FEATURES ARE DARK, SLIGHTLY REDDISH, WITH PLEASING FACES AND NOSES, WELL BUILT. THEY WALK NAKED, WITH NO COVERING WHATSOEVER. THEY ARE AS UNASHAMED TO SHOW THEIR PRIVATE PARTS AS THEY ARE THEIR FACES. IN THIS RESPECT THEY ARE OF EXTREME INNOCENCE.(...)

THEY SEEM TO ME OF SUCH INNOCENCE THAT, IF THEY COULD UNDERSTAND OUR LANGUAGE AND US THEIRS, THEY WOULD SOON BE CHRISTIANS, GIVEN THAT THEY DO NOT HAVE, NEITHER UNDERSTAND, ANY BELIEF AT ALL, OR SO IT APPEARS.

AND ONE COULD EASILY IMPRINT UPON THEM WHATEVER CHARACTER ONE MAY DESIRE, (...).

BUT THIS CHARACTER TO BE SUPPOSEDLY IMPRINTED WAS IN FACT MORE LIKE A WEDGE. THROUGH THE INDIANS' WINDOW OF INNOCENCE AND CURIOSITY THE COLONIZERS' REAL PLANS WERE INTRODUCED THROUGH VIOLENCE: CONQUEST OF LAND, SLAVERY AND THE SUBJECTION OF PEOPLES TO NEW RELIGIOUS STRICTURES. THIS WAS WHAT THE PORTUGUESE WERE REALLY OFFERING THE INDIANS: ONE TRAVAIL, ONE BOSS, ONE GOD. FOR THE PLURALITY AND FREEDOM OF THE INDIGENOUS UNIVERSE THIS WAS THE SAME AS DEATH.

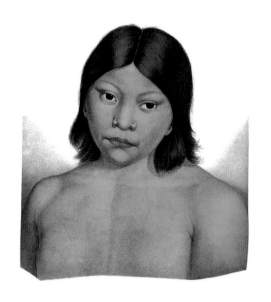
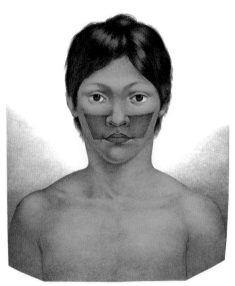

13

THE WORLD
BELONGED
TO THEM.

THE FIRST EXCHANGES.

IN THE FIRST YEARS OF THE 16TH CENTURY, THE FUTURE DID NOT SEEM SO DARK FOR THESE PEOPLE. THE CARAVELS HAD ONLY JUST ARRIVED WHEN THE INDIANS BEGAN TO ORGANIZE THEMSELVES FOR THE GENERAL PILLAGE: BRAZIL-WOOD TREES IN EXCHANGE FOR IRON TOOLS AND MIRRORS; UNMARRIED WOMEN OFFERED AS WIVES FOR THE WHITES WHO DECIDED TO STAY. THIS WAS THE IN-LAW SYSTEM THAT ACCORDING TO THE SOCIAL STRUCTURE OF THE NATIVE PEOPLE STRENGTHENED AND GAVE GREATER INFLUENCE TO THE TRIBES. MIXED MARRIAGE ALLOWED THE GRADUAL DISMANTLING OF THE COASTAL TRIBES AND THE BIRTH OF A MIXED-RACE, BRAZIL-INDIAN, MESTIZO PEOPLE: THE FACE OF BRAZIL.

THE MESTIZO CHILDREN, BROUGHT UP IN THE SETTLEMENTS OF THE WHITES, WITH THE ANCESTRAL KNOWLEDGE OF THEIR MOTHERS AND THE CONQUERING MENTALITY OF THEIR FATHERS, FORMED THE MOST DEVASTATING ARMY OF HUNTERS OF INDIANS IN THE FOLLOWING DECADES. HISTORY WOULD LATER CALL THEM BANDEIRANTES.

TAKING ADVANTAGE OF INTER-TRIBAL DISPUTES OVER TERRITORY, EXTREMELY BITTER IN THE 17TH CENTURY, THESE MESTIZO BANDEIRANTES REGIMENTED THOUSANDS OF INDIANS FROM THEIR "FAMILIES" AND SOCIAL GROUPS, YOUNG WARRIORS

FULL OF THE DESIRE TO FIGHT, AND LEAD THEM OUT ON SLAVE RAIDS ON OTHER INDIANS, LOOKING FOR GOLD OR SIMPLY ADVENTURE. THE RESULT OF THESE BANDEIRANTE ADVENTURES REPRESENTED, NOT ONLY MASS EXTERMINATION, BUT ALSO THE FORCED MIXTURE OF FLEEING PEOPLES SEEKING SHELTER IN THE FARTHEST-FLUNG REACHES OF BRAZIL: A LOSS OF A HUMAN CONTINGENT AND CULTURAL HERITAGE.

"This never-before seen massacre was the fruit of a complex process the agents of which were men and microorganisms but whose engines can be reduced to two: greed and ambition, cultural forms of expansion that were conventionally known as mercantile capitalism. Miserly motives and not a deliberate policy of extermination achieved the shocking result of reducing a population in the millions in 1500 to the scant 200,000 Indians today living in Brazil."

(Manuela Carneiro da Cunha. A História dos Índios no Brasil)

Xikrin, Xingu-MT ©F. Golfman

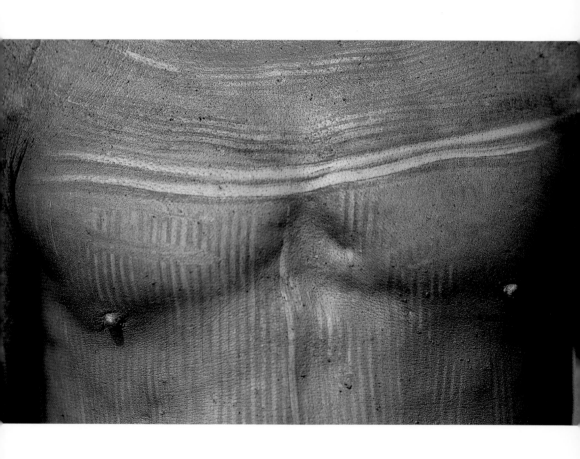

THE COMPANY OF JESUS.

THE BROTHERS OF THE COMPANY OF JESUS ALSO PLAYED THEIR PART IN THE RAPID DETERIORATION OF THE INDIGENOUS COSMOS. THE COMPANY HAD BEEN FOUNDED IN EUROPE ONLY NINE YEARS BEFORE, WHEN IN 1549 TOMÉ DE SOUZA ARRIVED IN BAHIA. THEY WERE MISSIONARIES AND SAW IN THE "PURITY" OF THE INDIAN FERTILE GROUND FOR THEIR WORK. SPREADING FROM THE NORTH OF THE COUNTRY TO THE SOUTH, THEY GROUPED THOUSANDS OF INDIANS INTO "REDOUBTS" OR MISSIONS UNDER THEIR TUTELAGE, WHERE THEY WERE ORGANIZED TO PROVIDE LABOR AND BE CONVERTED. THOUSANDS UPON THOUSANDS OF INDIANS FELL VICTIM TO THE WHITE MAN'S DISEASES, TO WHICH THEY HAD NO IMMUNITY. CONCENTRATED AND DEFENSELESS, THEY WERE ALSO EASY PREY TO THE FURY OF THE BANDEIRANTES. "GENERALLY SPEAKING, THE JESUITS FOCUSSED THEIR STRATEGY ON THREE AREAS: CONVERSION OF THE PRINCIPAL LEADERS, INDOCTRINATION OF THE YOUNG AND THE ELIMINATION OF THE SHAMANS" (JOHN MANUEL MONTEIRO). OR AS JORGE CALDEIRA WOULD RE-ITERATE, THE CO-OPTION OF POLITICAL POWER, THE CONTROL OF EDUCATION AND THE SUPPRESSION OF ANY COMPETITION IN QUESTIONS OF FAITH (IN A NAÇÃO MERCANTILISTA).

FROM THE BEGINNING THE JESUIT PRESENCE AND THEIR CONTROL OVER THE INDIANS WAS EXTREMELY INCONVENIENT FOR THE COLONIZERS AND EVEN FOR THE FATHERS OF OTHER CATHOLIC ORDERS UNABLE TO MAINTAIN THEIR CELIBACY IN THE MIDST OF THE INDIANS. DIVERGENCES BETWEEN THEM RESULTED IN SERIOUS CONFLICT, LEADING TO THEIR EXPULSION FROM SÃO PAULO IN 1540 (ONLY TO RETURN IN 1653) AND FROM MARANHÃO IN 1661. IF IT HAD DEPENDED ONLY ON THE COLONISTS, LIFE IN BRAZIL WOULD HAVE BEEN DELIGHTFULLY POLYGAMOUS, EXPLOITATIVE AND SLAVE-BASED.

THE MODUS VIVENDI:

ALTHOUGH THERE WERE SO MANY LINGUISTIC DIFFERENCES BETWEEN THE INDIGENOUS PEOPLES OF BRAZIL, THERE WERE ALSO SIGNIFICANT PARALLELS IN THE TRIBES' "MODUS VIVENDI". ALMOST ALL HAD NO FIXED TERRITORY; THEY CONSTANTLY SOUGHT NEW LANDS FOR CULTIVATION DURING THEIR WANDERINGS AND NEW HUNTING GROUNDS WHEN THEY IT DEEMED NECESSARY. ON ACCOUNT OF THIS MOBILITY THE COMMUNAL LIVING QUARTERS WERE BUILT TO BE IMPERMANENT AND THE ACCUMULATION OF WEALTH, POSSESSIONS AND PRODUCTS SIMPLY OUT OF THE QUESTION. THE INDIANS BUILT NEITHER CITIES NOR FORTIFICATIONS WITH WHICH TO DEFEND THEMSELVES, AND DID NOT SEE THE LAND AS SOMETHING TO BE POSSESSED: AFTER ALL NO ONE COULD OWN THAT WHICH HAS ITS OWN SOUL, THAT WHICH IS SELF-POSSESSED. IT WAS THUS THAT THEY SAW THE WIND, THE RIVERS AND RAINS: BEINGS WITH THEIR OWN SOULS. THE INDIAN AND HIS SOUL WERE SIMPLY ONE PART OF A UNIVERSE OF MANY OTHER SOULS. THEN CAME THE PORTUGUESE...

" Indigenous peoples always thought
that the land and everything in the land
was their responsibility to protect.
We feel that we are responsible for the things
that happen". Ailton Krenak

THE FIRE IN THE CENTER OF THE LONG-HUT BROUGHT REMEMBRANCE WHILE THE STORIES OF THE ELDERS INTERPRETED FOR THE YOUNG PEOPLE ALL THE EVENTS OF THEIR LIVES AND THEIR PEOPLE'S HISTORY. IT WAS, AND STILL IS, THROUGH A COMPLEX MYTHOLOGY THAT THE INDIGENOUS PEOPLES OF BRAZIL EXPLAIN THEIR WORLD, INCLUDING THAT WORLD THAT HAS CHANGED SO MUCH SINCE THE ARRIVAL OF THE WHITE MAN.

"The meetings at which myths were recounted above all took place on occasions determined by natural cycles: the dry or wet seasons, the time of planting or harvesting, the period of abundant or scarce game. These were sacred moments. In order to hear the myths, the audience had to be removed from their daily routine. Special vestments were used (...). Meals were also different; alcoholic beverages and teas were partaken of and special herbs smoked. With normal routine suspended, the passage of time was marked by music, invocations and collective dancing." *

THE ABOVE DESCRIPTION COULD STILL BE USED TODAY WITHOUT CHANGING ANYTHING, FOR CARNIVAL IN SALVADOR OR RIO DE JANEIRO, THE FESTIVAL OF THE BULL IN PARINTINS (AM) AND SO MANY OTHER BRAZILIAN CELEBRATIONS. THE VESTMENTS, DRINKS AND HERBS MAY HAVE CHANGED, AND THE MYTHS MAY HAVE RETREATED INTO THE COLLECTIVE SUBCONSCIOUS OF BRAZIL, BUT IT CANNOT BE DENIED THAT AS LEGITIMATE DESCENDANTS OF INDIANS, WE ARE ALWAYS IN SEARCH OF A ROUTE OUT OF THE EVERYDAY WORLD INTO, IF NOT A MYTHOLOGICAL WORLD, AT LEAST ONE THAT IS MAGICAL.

* *Viagem pela História do Brasil*, of Jorge Caldeira, Flávio de Carvalho, Cláudio Marcondes and Sérgio Goes de Paula.

Xavantes-MT ©R. Faquini

For this reason if you hear an Indian speaking less-than-perfect

Portuguese on TV, it should be remembered that

what is everyday vernacular for us

is an imposed and foreign language for him.

The Indians speak many languages, do you?

For this reason, if you think it strange that today

their reserves cover 10% of Brazil's territory, remember:

before your great-great-great-great-grandfather arrived,

all this belonged to his great-great-great-great-grandfather,

and was not yet called Brazil. The Brazilian government

recognizes the right of land ownership to any citizen

who has lived on it for more than five years.

The Indians arrived many thousands of years ago.

FOR THIS REASON, WHEN YOU BATHE SEVERAL TIMES A DAY,

WHEN YOU SWING TO THE RHYTHM OF A HAMMOCK,

WHEN YOU CONVERSE AROUND A CAMPFIRE,

WHEN YOU PAUSE TO LISTEN TO THE WIND,

WHEN YOU, AS AN ADULT, LAUGH AND PLAY LIKE A CHILD,

OR WHEN YOU EAT AS IF THERE WERE NO TOMORROW UNTIL YOUR STOMACH HURTS,

WHEN YOU LOVE AND RESPECT CHILDREN OR LOVE AND RESPECT YOUR ELDERS,

WHEN YOU HEAR A BIRD'S SONG AND DISCOVER ITS NAME,

WHEN YOU VENERATE THE EARTH AS A MOTHER AND A DAUGHTER,

AND WHEN YOU SEE A CRYSTAL-CLEAR STREAM AND OVERFLOW WITH HAPPINESS,

AND WHEN YOU TREAT NATURE WELL,

YOU SEE THE INDIAN IN YOURSELF.

HE WHO SETS FIRE TO AN INDIAN, SETS FIRE TO HIMSELF.

PORTO CALE. The European root.

Well before the Christian era, even eleven centuries after its beginning, there was no Portugal, but rather a loose series of dominions over the peoples inhabiting the western extremities of the Iberian peninsula. The Romans stayed for seven centuries, set up the first public institutions, implemented market agriculture and planted the first seeds of local trade, until, in the fifth century their empire collapsed throughout Europe. The Arabs arrived in 711AD and only finally left Europe at the end of the 15th century. In the region that was to become Portugal, they stayed for five hundred years, making fundamental alterations to the formation of the people and their society. They spread their culture founding schools and libraries; expanded production with industries manufacturing textiles, arms, tiles and leather; and, a valuable gift, left them the first navigational techniques. By mixing with the original inhabitants they darkened the future Portuguese people.

And above all, the Moors forged in the sentiments of the people, in the iron and blood of humiliation, a mythical sword ever ready to cut off the head of the infidel.

With the Moorish domination, the wounds of Christ became the wounds of Portugal: ever since, their meetings with other non-Christian peoples was if putting a finger in the wound.

It was with the coming of barbarians from the north, principally Visigoths during the late Roman Empire, and later during the struggle to expel the Moors, that the essence of the peoples of the peninsula was formed: Hispania, which in Latin signified "the lands to the west". During almost the whole period of Moorish presence, the term Portugal referred only to little Porto Cale, a settlement on the banks of the River Douro, extending to the River Lima, a county belonging to the Hispanic kingdom of Galicia: a small fief with independent ideas ever since its creation.

The year is 1050. In the middle of the period of the Crusades, while the armies of Europe threw themselves into the re-conquest of the holy places, such as Jerusalem, captured by the Arabs, there was still an unwelcome Arab presence in the Iberian peninsula. Alphonso VI, King of Leon and Castille, while fighting to expel the infidel from his lands, requested military assistance from the French, German and Nordic crusaders. The deal signed, two powerful armies were sent by the Cluny Abbey of France and victory finally won. Porto Cale and the hand of Dona Thereza, the king's daughter, were the prizes given to Henry of Burgundy, one of the most famous knights of the Holy Wars. On taking possession of his lands,

Henry was made aware of the separatist dreams of his Portuguese subjects, a dream in agreement with his own desire for suzerainty. The next generation of this nascent dynasty from Burgundy found its freedom by winning independence once and for all. D. Alphonso I, Henry of Burgundy's son, would become the first "rex portucallensis".

Left page: Pirenopolis-GO ©R. Faquini / Salvador-BA ©Saulo Kainuma

The murals of Nuno Gonçalves were completed in 1460 and portray the beginnings of Portugal's overseas expansion. Personages from the entire kingdom

were portrayed: the King, the Queen, Crown Prince Henry, bankers, knights, monks and even sailors, the faces of Portugal yesterday and today.

PORTUGAL'S GREATEST ACHIEVEMENT:
RESISTING CASTILLE.

Porto Cale or Portugal, always one step ahead of the world's affairs, became one of the first kingdoms in Europe to set sail out of the Middle Ages and into modern times. The centuries of fighting the Moors had given the people a common purpose, unity. Portugal assumed its modern shape in 1249 by taking possession of all the Algarve. They had faced plagues, overcome crises and, above all, they had managed to avoid succumbing to the pressures of Castille.

After unification, another two centuries of preparation were still needed for Portugal to hoist her sails and gain the ocean. They began with the conquest of a spiritual world.

THE POWER OF THE SPIRIT.

Under D. Dinis (1261-1325), Portugal flourished as an agricultural and fishing kingdom, trading its surpluses. However, it was principally souls that the king was interested in fishing and cultivating. It was with his backing that the ideas of the monk Joaquim de Flora (1145-1202) swept the country. They preached an Era of the Holy Spirit, of total equality among men, after which would follow the Era of the Father (the time of Jehovah for the Jews) and the Era of the Son, and the evangelization of the whole world. In an attempt to avoid the persecution of Rome and the Pope who had excommunicated followers of the doctrine, D. Dinis and the Holy Queen Isabella (canonized in 1625), created the popular festivals of the Holy Spirit, apparently separated from official religion but pregnant with the symbols and myths of this new Era.

In each settlement where the festival of the Holy Spirit (created by the king 1261-1325, occurred, a poor and innocent boy was crowned emperor. On this day, the royal family and their court celebrated with their subjects, symbolizing with this the possibility of a classless society. Much food was distributed evoking the meaning of abundance. Lastly, prisoners were released, showing a burning desire for a peaceful society free of crime.

The action of the Inquisition would later spell the end of these festivals in Portugal.

D. Dinis, at the same as he held off pressure from the Pope and the King of France, gave his protection in Portugal to the wealthy and powerful Order of the Knights Templar, later renaming it the Order of Christ. Sponsored by this same order and in the name of Christ, two centuries later the Portuguese caravels would weigh anchor in search of new worlds.

Under the leadership of D. Dinis, Portugal grew stronger, as on Earth so in heaven: it was at one and the same time a mercantilist nation consolidating its trading and maritime bourgeoisie and a kingdom illuminated by Christian myths, a country of knights subscribing to the ideals of King Arthur, in search of its own Holy Grail.

D. Dinis set the country's territorial limits once and for all, made Portuguses the official language and initiated its maritime plans by planting the pine groves that would furnish the wood for its ships, and contracted Genovese sea captains who brought with them the knowledge that would lay the foundations for the next generation at the naval school at Sagres.

The following generations of kings (and I am now summarizing the story), gradually came to look upon the seas more as a source of riches rather than as a holy mission. They fought for their sovereignty with faith. The Revolution of Avis (1383-1385), for example, was a struggle involving everybody – nobles, bourgeoisie and people – against Castille, and culminated in the consolidation of the bourgeois traders. For this reason, guided by mercantilism, they no longer looked in the distance no for the Golden Age, the Greek myth of equality between men, but for the inequality that gold would bring.

"With the death of D. Duarte (1438), (...), then
D. Afonso V(1472) (...), comes the time of D. João II.
And when a political man thinks there are times
to fly like a falcon and other times to fly like an owl,
yet without even a word of remembrance
for the mystical dove of Portugal, for that symbol
of the Holy Spirit, consoler of men, which entered
Portuguese history with Queen Isabel (...),
this man may have such grandeur that time
tires not in praising; he may have fulfilled
the mission given to him in this world;
he may have been the admirable representative
of a large mass of an epoch's citizens;
yet there hangs over him a fatal condemnation:
he worshipped not God but golden calves;
betrayed the nation in its essence... (...).
It is precisely with D.João II that the gap
that was English and anti-Catholic widens.
And, through that gap...
everything is destroyed that could have been
extraordinary in the Middle Ages: in such a way
that it could be said that Portugal, after the 15th century,
will only achieve greatness in that which continues
to be medieval; in other matters she is diminished."*

PORTUGAL AND THE CONQUEST OF THE WORLD.

With power in the hands of the Avis Dynasty, principally during the reign of D. João II, known as the "Perfect Prince", the Portuguese lost a little of heaven, won a whole lot of sea, and revealed a world that was much bigger than ever before imagined. They took Ceuta (1415) in north Africa, conquered the islands of Madeira (1418/19), then the Azores (1427/28) leaving the way open to the west coast of Africa, reaching the Indies and finally Brazil. In 1494, in an act of unparalleled arrogance, Portugal divided the world in half with Spain in the Treaty of Tordesillas.

THE PORTUGUESE LEGACY.

Vieira said one hundred and fifty years after the Discovery that the Portuguese governors desired not our wellbeing but only our wealth. It's undeniable, that they left in the land, (or perhaps in the air...) a smell of individualism, a kind of each man for himself, an uncomfortable characteristic that can be seen even today.

But those that came here only to take were not the only ones, let alone the first. Other Portuguese that took refuge in Brazil – colonists searching for a new start, deserters from ships unwilling to return to Portugal, those fleeing persecution in Europe on religious or ethnic grounds – brought with them the precious and ancient legacy of the House of Burgundy.

The festivities of the Holy Spirit, the jousting tournaments between Christians and Moors, the hopeful return of D. Sebastian, missing in Africa fighting the infidel, and who would bring with him a period of equality between men, faded in Portugal but flourished in Brazil.

The spiritual (whether holy or not) is the richest part of our Portuguese heritage.

And also, as Loren McIntyre, the book's photographer, has remarked, the desire to sing for whatever reason, whether good or bad, this worship of the Virgin Mary or perhaps just Marys, this compulsion to decorate life with garlands and the courage to confront sea monsters even without knowing how to swim... This light-hearted spirit of ours as a nation that gives flight to our imagination, all had its origin in Portugal.

* Reflection of Agostinho da Silva. Extract from the book *Museu Aberto do Descobrimento - O Brasil Renasce Onde Nasce*. Organized by Roberto Pinho

THE PORTUGUESE HERITAGE: FREE-SPIRITED, THE EYES GAZING OUT TO SEA.

(...) And for the immense and possible ocean,
As taught within the following refrain,
although the inland sea be Greek or Roman,
the open sea is Portugal's domain

God wills, man dreams, the work is born
God wished the earth to be as one.
That the ocean should unite rather than divide.
You consecrated yourself and set off through the spray,

And the white shoreline went from island to continent,
Whitening further until the end of the world.
And suddenly an entire land was sighted,
Rising, whole, from the depths of blue.

The Lord who blessed thee made thee Portuguese
From the sea, and in thee brought forth us all
The sea was true; the empire treacherous
Oh God, where is the glory that is Portugal

THE REIGN OF OLODUMARÉ.
AFRICAN ROOTS.

15TH CENTURY. PORTUGAL HAD LONG HAD HER SIGHTS SET ON ISLAMIC, MEDITERRANEAN AFRICA FOR THE OLD RELIGIOUS AND EXPANSIONIST REASONS. HOWEVER, IT WAS PRINCE HENRY THE NAVIGATOR WHO PROPELLED PORTUGAL TO GO FURTHER AFIELD, ALONG THE COAST OF THE STILL-UNKNOWN CONTINENT. IT WAS AS A PRESENT FOR PRINCE HENRY THAT THE CARAVELS BROUGHT BACK THE FIRST BLACK SLAVES FROM AFRICA. IT WAS THE BEGINNING OF THE OVERSEAS TRADE IN HUMANS THAT WOULD CONTINUE FOR THE NEXT FOUR HUNDRED YEARS.

Previous pages, left: Pirenópolis-GO ©R. Linsker; right: Salvador-BA ©Aristides A.; Salvador-BA ©Aristides A.; Boninal-BA ©R. Linsker; Camamu-BA ©R. Linsker

A BLACK BALANCE SHEET. IN THE EARLY YEARS, FROM 1441 TO 1446, ONE THOUSAND SLAVES WERE BROUGHT BACK TO LISBON FROM THEN UNTIL THE END OF THE CENTURY, FIVE HUNDRED SLAVES WOULD ARRIVE ANNUALLY MODEST NUMBERS COMPARED TO THOSE BROUGHT TO BRAZIL AS OF THE MID-16TH CENTURY WITH THE SCARCITY OF LABOR IN THE SUGAR PLANTATIONS OF THE BRAZILIAN NORTHEAST – THOUSANDS OF INDIANS WORKING IN THE SUGAR CANE FIELDS HAD FALLEN VICTIM TO EPIDEMICS – THE SUGAR BARONS WERE FORCED TO IMPORT SLAVES FROM THE GUINEA COAST FOUR MILLION WERE BROUGHT TO BRAZIL OVER THE NEXT THREE HUNDRED YEARS, UNTIL THE TRADE WAS ABOLISHED IN 1850 THIS WITHOUT COUNTING ANOTHER FOUR MILLION WHO PERISHED IN THE "MIDDLE PASSAGE" AND WERE SIMPLY THROWN OVERBOARD

LIVES FOR RIFLES. SLAVERY IS AS OLD AS MAN WHEN THE FIRST PORTUGUESE CARAVELS WERE REACHING AFRICA IN THE 15TH CENTURY, IT WAS HARDLY RARE FOR THE LOCAL KINGS TO OWN SLAVES, ENEMIES TAKEN PRISONER IN TRIBAL DISPUTES SEEING AN OPPORTUNITY FOR CHEAP LABOR IN A PORTUGAL THAT LACKED HANDS IN AGRICULTURE AND THE MORE DEGRADING TRADES, THE PORTUGUESE OFFERED THE KINGS CHEAP KNICK-KNACKS AND PROPOSED ALLIANCES AND SO THE INCIPIENT TRADE IN SLAVES WAS SETTLED LIVES IN EXCHANGE FOR KNICK-KNACKS, RIFLES, VIRTUALLY NOTHING WHILE

IN EUROPE PORTUGAL WAS BECOMING ONE OF THE NATIONS MOST PREPARED FOR CONQUEST, AFRICAN MONARCHS RUSHED TO THE BACKLANDS TO CAPTURE PEOPLE, TEARING THE CONTINENT APART IN FRATRICIDAL WARS THE PRINCIPAL PORTS OF EMBARKATION WERE SENEGAL, BENIN, NIGERIA, THE ISLAND OF SÃO THOMÉ, GUINEA, ANGOLA E MOZAMBIQUE KINGDOMS WERE CREATED OR EXPANDED THROUGH THIS ALLIANCE WITH PORTUGAL DAHOMEY, BENIN, AND OTHERS IN 1890, FOR EXAMPLE, 94% OF ANGOLA'S INCOME CAME FROM THE SLAVE TRADE WITH BRAZIL SO GREAT WAS THE CONNECTION BETWEEN THESE COUNTRIES, THAT WITH BRAZIL'S INDEPENDENCE IN 1822, A MOVEMENT WAS BEGUN FOR THE UNION OF THE COLONY WITH BRAZIL RATHER THAN PORTUGAL

EMBASSIES OF SUFFERING. IN 1482 PORTUGAL HAD ALREADY BUILT THE FORTRESS OF SÃO JORGE DE MINA, ON THE COAST OF THE GULF OF GUINEA OTHERS WOULD FOLLOW, SUCH AS THAT OF AJUDÁ IN BENIN THESE IMMENSE FORTIFIED CASTLES FUNCTIONED AS EMBASSIES AND CENTERS OF TRADE BETWEEN COUNTRIES FORTRESSES BUILT BY THE PORTUGUESE, FRENCH AND ENGLISH LINED THE WHOLE COAST OF AFRICA AJUDÁ WAS ENTIRELY PAID FOR BY SLAVE TRADERS FROM BAHIA IN BRAZIL WHO AT THIS POINT, AND UNTIL THE ABOLITION OF SLAVERY IN 1850, REPRESENTED AN

EXTREMELY POWERFUL ECONOMIC POWER IN COLONIAL BRAZIL. THE FORTRESSES, IN ADDITION TO ALLOWING THE TRADERS PROXIMITY TO THEIR MERCHANDISE, PERMITTED A GREATER ECONOMY OF SCALE. SHIPS ARRIVED WITH RUM, TOBACCO AND CONCH SHELLS, RETURNING IMMEDIATELY WITH THEIR HOLDS CRAMMED FULL OF ENSLAVED AFRICANS. PORTUGUESE POLICY IN TERMS OF MAINTAINING CONTROL OVER THE REGION WAS THE SAME AS THAT IN THE BRAZILIAN COLONIES. THE ORDER OF THE DAY WAS TO PROCREATE IN ORDER TO GOVERN ALLIANCES WITH THE LOCAL KINGS WERE COMMONLY MADE THROUGH INTER-RACIAL MARRIAGES. SOCIAL LIFE AND BUSINESS. EVERYTHING HAPPENED AROUND THE SLAVING FORTRESSES.

THE TREE OF FORGETFULNESS. MEN SOLD THEIR BROTHERS FROM NEARBY TRIBES, ALTHOGH WITH SUCH FEAR OF THE POWER OF THE CURSES OF THOSE WHO WERE LEAVING, THAT THEY TOOK SHIFTS IN PRAYING ON THE BEACH FOR THE CURSES TO BE DISSIPATED ON THE WIND. LEGEND HAS IT THAT IN A SLAVE EXPORTING COUNTRY, THERE WAS A LARGE SOLITARY TREE ON THE ROAD TO THE PORT* LOCAL BELIEF HAD IT THAT IF EACH MALE SLAVE WALKED AROUND THE TREE NINE TIMES, AND EACH WOMAN SEVEN, THEN THOUGHTS OF THEIR COUNTRY, THEIR ROOTS AND THEIR SUFFERING WOULD BE WIPED FROM THEIR MEMORIES. THEY WOULD THEN BE LEFT WITHOUT THE STRENGTH TO REBEL ON THE SEA PASSAGE AND IN THE NEW COUNTRIES TO

WHICH THEY WERE TAKEN. THE TREE BETRAYED THE BETRAYERS: NOBODY FORGOT BRAZIL. THUS BECAME PART AFRICAN. THANKS ALSO TO A TREE THAT LET NO ONE FORGET THE ROOTS OF THEIR IDENTITY. AS SOON AS THEY ARRIVED, THE SURVIVING SLAVES WERE BAPTIZED. THE CHURCH OF THE TIME CONNIVED WITH THE TRADE AND JUSTIFIED IT WITH THE CHRISTIANIZATION OF SOULS THAT, IF LEFT IN AFRICA, WOULD HAVE REMAINED IN PERDITION. THE FUSION OF THE MOST SACRED – THE NAMES OF THE SAINTS – WITH THE MOST PROFANE – THE TRAFFIC IN LIVES – OCCURRED ON THE SLAVE SHIPS. NAMED AFTER SAINTS. "SAINT JOSEPH" WAS DESERVING OF GREAT DEVOTION ON THE SLAVE SHIPS, AND AROUND 1757 ACHIEVED THE STATUS OF PRIVATE PROTECTOR OF THOSE BUSINESSMEN DEVOTING THEMSELVES TO THE SLAVE TRADE ON THE MINA COAST. (...) THIS EASE OF CONSCIENCE ON THE SLAVE SHIPS WAS TOTAL. AROUND 1890, VARIOUS MERCHANTS ESTABLISHED IN ANGOLA SOLICITED THE KING OF PORTUGAL EXILED IN BRAZIL AS OF 1808, RECOMPENSE FOR THE ZEAL EXHIBITED BY THEM IN THIS KIND OF ACTIVITY**

Salvador-BA ©Aristides A.

(...)
YESTERDAY SIERRA LEONE,
WAR, LION HUNTING,
SLEEPING UNDER THE TENTS OF AMPLITUDE!
TODAY... THE BLACK HOLD, DEEP,
INFECTED, CRAMPED, FILTHY,
WITH THE PLAGUE CREEPING STEALTHILY
AS A JAGUAR...
AND SLEEP ALWAYS TRUNCATED BY A CORPSE
BEING THROWN OVERBOARD,
THE SLAP OF THE BODY AS IT HIT THE WATER...

YESTERDAY COMPLETE FREEDOM,
THE DESIRE FOR POWER...
TODAY... THE DEPTHS OF EVIL,
NOT EVEN FREE TO DIE...
CLAMP THEM TO THE SAME CHAIN
- LUGUBRIOUS IRON SNAKE -
THE SCREWS OF SLAVERY.
AND THUS, MOCKING DEATH,
DANCES THE LUGUBRIOUS COURT
TO THE SOUND OF THE WHIP... MOCKERY!

THERE IS A PEOPLE THAT USES THE FLAG TO
COVER SO MUCH INFAMY AND COWARDICE!...
AND THEY TURN IT IN THIS FIESTA
INTO THE STAINED CLOAK
OF A COLD BACCHANALIAN!...
OH MY GOD! MY GOD! BUT WHAT FLAG IS THIS
THAT IMPUDENTLY TREMBLES ON THE MAST?
SILENCE. MUSE... WEEP, AND WEEP SUCH THAT
THE PAVILION IS BATHED IN YOUR TEARS! ...

GOLDEN GREEN PENDANT OF MY LAND,
THAT THE BREEZE OF BRAZIL KISSES AND MOVES,
STANDARD TO WHICH THE SUNLIGHT PUTS AN END
AND THE DIVINE PROMISES OF HOPE...
YOU THAT, FROM THE LIBERTY
WON THROUGH WAR,
WAS HOISTED ON THE LANCE-TIP OF HEROES
RATHER THAT YOU HAD ROTTED IN BATTLE,
THAN BE USED AS A NATION'S SHROUD!...

(NAVIO NEGREIRO. CASTRO ALVES)

THE CULT OF REMEMBRANCE: SINCRETISM. Slaves were not allowed to take their belongings with them. What remained was the baggage of memory. And the exercise of this remembrance was slowly made possible through disguised cult. Perhaps due to similar purposes or the identification of some common symbol, the African deities – the orixás –, came to be identified with the Catholic saints. Xangô, god of thunder, was linked to Saint Geronimo, as the saint had a lion at his feet. Obaluaê, god of smallpox, was identified with Saint Lazarus as their bodies were both covered in wounds. The goddess Iemanjá came alive as Our Lady of Conception and Ogun hunted and fought as Saint George. The masters were almost always indulgent with the mixed practices of the slave-quarters. On Sundays they were allowed to dance to the sound of the drums. " The latter (the masters), seeing their slaves dancing according to their habits and singing in their own language, judged that they were witnessing nothing but nostalgic Africans having fun. They did not suspect that they were singing prayers and worshipping their orixás, their vodun, their inkissi". (Pierre Fatumbi Verger. Os Orixás). People from many different tribes came to Brazil, bringing with them many different Africas. Peoples with differing customs, languages and religions. So as not to lose their common cultural ties, the ethnic groups attempted to maintain their unity through the cults. In the Salvador of the 18th and 19th centuries, the blacks from Angola frequented the church of Rosario in Pelourinho square. Those from Dahomey worshipped in the Chapel of Corpus Sanctus in the lower town. The Nago people from Nigeria, through their brotherhoods, worshipped Our Lady of Good Fortune (the women) and Our Lord of Martyrs (the men). **ORIXÁ AND OLODUMARÉ.** The Orixás, divinities and deities were, for the people of Africa, their ancestors, achieving a special degree of power, a state of pure energy. A force that fused with everything and that was perceptible and could be made accessible to humans through possession by the spirit. The heads of clans and families (the balés) usually delegated responsibility for the cult to an aláàse, guardians of the power of God. These aláàse were assisted by the èlèguns, people with the ability to incorporate the orixás. Olodumaré, the maximum manifestation of God, was above the comprehension and reach of mortals. In this sense, the Orixás were the link between mere men and the great God. **WORK AND DEATH; LIFE AND FREEDOM.** The sugar mills were factories that killed the workers and enriched the sugar barons. During the period of production, they worked twenty-four hours a day, a presage of the industrial work shift of modern times. On average, slaves managed to live for a further eight to ten years after their arrival in Brazil. Any slacking was severely punished. Work in the gold mines was no less punishing. Experienced in the handling and smelting of precious metals, tens of thousands ended their lives in the mines. To the extent that they began to be integrated into life in the colony, flight began to be a real possibility. In the 17th and 18th centuries fugitives from justice, escaped slaves and other outcasts founded the first quilombos, or communities of escaped slaves, in the backlands of the interior. The Quilombo of Palmares was the greatest of these. It was located in the southern part of the province of Pernambuco, the modern-day state of Alagoas, in the Serra da Barriga mountain range. Around 1670, it is estimated that it was home to 20,000 people, split into five communities. At the beginning led by Ganga Zumba, Palmares was soon to feel the strength of Zumbi, a warrior who put the quilombo on a military footing and refused any peace overtures from the government. Zumbi's tactics for growth were to kidnap slaves from nearby plantations and then ambush their pursuers. In 1694, the bandeirante Domingos Jorge Velho and a large military force managed to destroy Palmares. Zumbi died almost two years later, betrayed by a trusted associate, and passed into Brazilian history as a symbol of black resistance. **THE BLACK LEGACY.** A sad history that of Brazil, which until 1850, when the slave trade was finally abolished, was a country basing its economic life on the exploitation of human life. Rui Barbosa, whether due to shame, remorse or as a cover-up, in 1891 burned all official archives relating to slavery, thereby destroying a significant part of Brazilian history. With the Aurea Law that abolished slavery in Brazil, a small percentage of Brazilian blacks returned to their countries of origin in Africa. The vast majority remained. Words such as quitute (delicacy), cafuné (tactile affection), remelexo (swing), batuque (beat of the drums) became rooted in Brazil: spicy cuisine, physical affection, sensual dance and hypnotic music. "In the tenderness, the excessive mimicry, in the Catholicism in which our senses delight, in the music, the way of walking, in speech, in children's lullabies, in everything that is a sincere expression of life, we carry the mark of our African heritage". Gilberto Freyre. Just to remind ourselves of the black mouth we have, Just to feel the black body that we express, Just to float in the black soul we possess, I whisper to you low and delicate my nego, my nega. The spice of Brazil is Africa.

  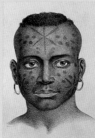 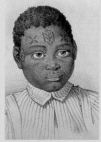 

TRUNK

The Tree that sustains us: Faith

" BETTER TO TRUST IN GOD THAN IN A PIECE OF WOOD".

THIS IS THE STORY OF A WELL-INTENTIONED HOAX, OF A CROOKED DEAL OR PERHAPS A FALSE TRUTH THAT OCCURRED IN BRAZIL, A LAND WHERE NOT EVERYTHING IS AS IT SEEMS, OR AT LEAST THAT IS WHAT WE WOULD LIKE TO BELIEVE.

"THE MAN RETURNED HOME AFTER DAYS AWAY, WHEN, STARTLED, HE REMEMBERED THAT HE HAD NOT BROUGHT WITH HIM A PIECE OF WOOD FROM THE CROSS OF A PARTICULAR CHURCH, HELD TO BE MIRACULOUS, AT THE SPECIAL REQUEST OF HIS WIFE. AND JUST WHEN HIS WIFE WAS UNWELL AND WAS WAITING FOR THE WOOD TO GRATE AND MAKE TEA, COMPRESSES AND OTHER HEALING MEDICINE.

THE MAN WAS UNWILLING TO APPEAR UNGRATEFUL, WHEEDLING, INTERESTED ONLY IN HIS OWN AFFAIRS, ETC, ETC, SO HE HAD THE IDEA OF GETTING A PIECE OF WOOD FROM THE BOAT THAT MADE THE RIVER CROSSING, AND, KNIFE IN HAND, SLICED OFF A NICE PIECE, AND SIGHED, ALMOST WITH RELIEF.

ARRIVING AT HOME, HIS WIFE, SICK IN BED, WAS ALSO RELIEVED HE HADN'T FORGOTTEN THE PRESENT, THE LITTLE RELIC OF WOOD FROM THE CROSS.... THE WOMAN QUICKLY GOT WELL WITH THE TEA FROM THE SACRED WOOD SHAVING. THEN IT WAS THE NEIGHBOR'S TURN TO USE THE SACRED MEDICINE AND AFTER THAT A CHILD FROM THE NEIGHBORHOOD. AND SO THE CROSS WON FAME IN THE REGION.

THE MAN KEPT QUIET. EXCEPT INSIDE HIS HEAD, HIS THOUGHTS INSISTED: SINNER, SINNER. AS HIS WIFE'S HAPPINESS INCREASED, SO HE BECAME SADDER. SHE WITH HER CHEEKS EVER ROSIER, HE WASTING AWAY.

UNTIL ONE DAY, CARRIED AWAY, HE BROKE DOWN AND BLURTED THAT THE WOOD WAS FAKE. THE WOMAN, THE NEIGHBOR AND THE CHILD ALL DIED WITHIN DAYS.

BETTER TO TRUST IN GOD THAN IN A PIECE OF WOOD.

Manaus-AM ©L. Principe

GOD IS BRAZILIAN.

Don't let on to the rest of the world,
but God is Brazilian. Or at least that's the conclusion
that Brazilians have reached, perhaps feeling blessed
with special emphasis on the higher spheres.
A joke? No. The subject is extremely serious and
mobilizes a country of diverse beliefs.
Within our diverse creeds and cultures we hold in
common a sentiment we can call... faith. But we could
also call it hope, optimism, good humor, a strong
predisposition to go ahead, despite the obstacles in the way,
as if some invisible being were holding our hand.

FAITH.

This invisible, impalpable agent perhaps makes
everything less concrete, more relative to our eyes.
Our famous goodwill, for example: we know better than most
how to reconcile antagonistic or opposing forces. For absolute
concepts such as good and evil, right and wrong,
well understood and duly separated in the rest of the world,
Brazil has invented a scale of gradations. Instead of a liar,
therefore, somebody has "distorted the facts" or even "was
mistaken". We tend toward easy euphemisms. We excuse
ourselves to excess (perhaps for this reason we hope that others
will not be so hard on us when we commit our little errors).

WE PLAY WITH FAITH.
AND WHEN WE ACHIEVE VICTORY,
WE INCLUDE GOD IN THE TEAM:

"THANKS BE TO GOD,
THE RESULT WAS POSITIVE AND..."

FAITH TRANSFORMS EVERYTHING: A GUITAR INTO A DRUM, SHAMANS INTO PRIESTS.

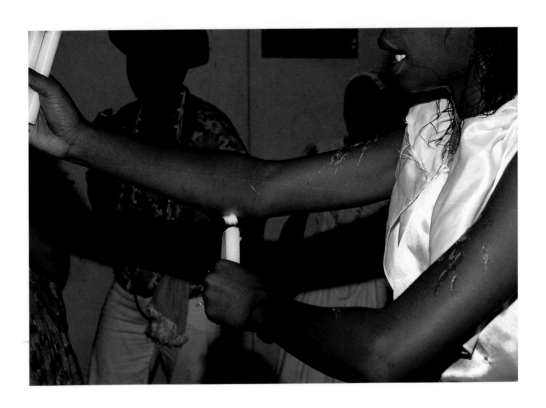

Soure-PA ©R. Linsker

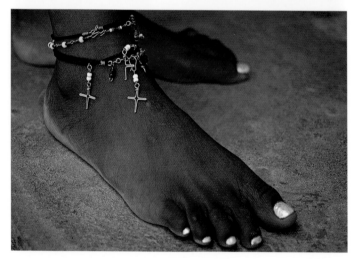

BEFORE ENTERING THE CULT'S MEETING PLACE TO RECEIVE THE SAINT'S SPIRIT, WE PUT ON ORNAMENTAL DRESS TO SHOW THAT GOD ON HIGH GUIDES OUR STEPS.

Atins-MA ©R. Linsker; Soure-PA ©R. Linsker   53

Left page: Crato-CE ©R. Linsker / Pantanal-MS ©F. Goifman; Serra do Divisor N.P.-AC ©R. Linsker; Barão de Melgaço-MS ©F. Goifman; Belém-PA ©P. Martinelli

LOOKING TO THE HEAVENS
WE ARE ILLUMINATED.

V O W S F U L F I L L E D .

EVERYTHING IN THIS BIZARRE BRAZIL IS APPROACHED IN A ROUNDABOUT WAY, AVOIDING THEREBY THE ARROW THRUST OF OBJECTIVITY: RACISM IS DISGUISED, PREJUDICE IS DIFFUSE, THE SOCIAL GULF HALF-HIDDEN. HOVERING IN THE AIR IS THE PROMISE THAT WE CAN SWITCH LANES, SCALE THE SOCIAL LADDER, CHANGE GROUPINGS. AND IN ORDER TO ATTAIN THIS BETTER LIFE, TO GET IT RIGHT, WE HOLD ON TO THE HOPE THAT WE CAN COUNT, AS ALREADY SAID, ON EXTRA HELP FROM ABOVE. WE PLEAD, PRAY, MAKE VOWS, THE LATTER BEING ONE OF THE MORE EFFECTIVE WAYS TO COERCE ANGELS AND SAINTS. FACED WITH MY SACRIFICE (THE VOW), THE SAINT (NICE FELLOW THAT HE IS), WILL BE INCAPABLE OF DENYING MY REQUEST: A MORE THAN REASONABLE LOGIC.

Left page: Diamantina-MG / Jericoacoara-CE; Santana do Cariri-CE; Santarém-PA; Rio Novo-MA ©R. Linsker

THANKS BE TO GOD. So much time spent pleading and praying (until 1820 the Catholic Church was the only officially permitted religion), led Brazilians to achieve substantial intimacy with the higher spheres. God is everywhere, but even so we continue our eternal search: pilgrimages, processions, prayers and devotion. And when God does His disappearing act, we attempt to understand that "God works in mysterious ways". God is also bizarre.

São Luis do Paraitinga-SP ©Ed Viggiani; São Francisco do Maranhão-MA ©R. Linsker; Serrinha-BA ©Aristides A.; Planaltina-DF ©Ed Viggiani; Ouro Preto-MG ©Ed Viggiani; Ouro Preto-MG ©Ed Viggiani; Juazeiro do Norte-CE ©Ed Viggiani.

FAITH IN WORK. HOWEVER, IT CANNOT BE SAID THAT BRAZIL LIVES ONLY FOR PARTYING, FOOTBALL AND RELIGION: OUR FAITH IN WORK ALWAYS MOVES US TO CHALLENGE OBSTACLES. WITH MORE COURAGE THAN PLANNING: WE INSIST ON TRYING TO CULTIVATE THE ARID BACKLANDS AND PRAY FOR RAIN INSTEAD OF BUILDING RESERVOIRS AND IRRIGATION SYSTEMS. WE ARE FOREVER EXPANDING OUR AGRICULTURAL FRONTIERS (DESTROYING INVALUABLE ECOSYSTEMS) AND WASTE FOOD IN GRAIN SILOS FOR LACK OF A DECENT DISTRIBUTION NETWORK. ALWAYS HEARD, THE DIVINE OBSERVATION: IN A COMMERCIAL ESTABLISHMENT THE VOICE OF THE WORKERS ASKS: "WITH GOD ON OUR SIDE, WHO CAN BE AGAINST US?" WHO INDEED?"

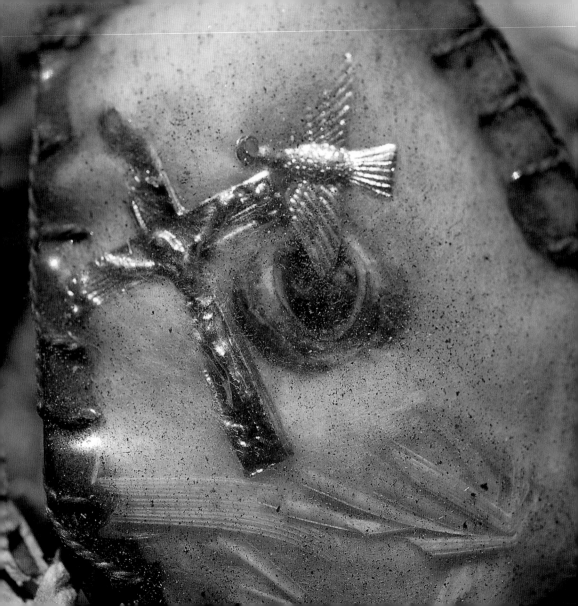

FAITH IN EVERYTHING. Such celestial intimacy sometimes reaches the height of absurdity. Such as when girls from the provinces wishing to find a husband take a statue of St. Anthony and torture him, turn him upside down, tie him up with cloth strips until he agrees to the little tyrants' wishes.

And when they say that God closes a door in order to open a window, Brazilians have learned the lesson well. If prayers in church aren't giving the right result, we can always go guiltlessly to a religious cult. On New Year's Eve, we migrate from midnight mass straight to a river or the sea, offer flowers and make our prayers to Iemanjá: an unprejudiced search for happiness.

Faith and Festivity come together and merge in this immense desire to be happy: the street festival, carnival, or when our team wins the soccer game, give us more than enough cause for optimism (and not to have to face that which is distasteful). On top of the carnival floats dressed in our fancy costumes, we are transformed into kings and queens and live a life where anything is permissible. "Let me kiss you right now, don't take offence, today is Carnival". In Carnival we transcend barriers of class, race and religion. Only for it all to end on Ash Wednesday.

Soccer, by the same token, gives us the chance several times a year to become champions and winners; happy, in the "brotherhood" that springs from bosses and employees, rich and poor. Supporters of the same team, we seem to share the same joys and sadness despite the distance separating our addresses and bank accounts. With what elan we pull down the barricades, destroy the symbols and confront the opponents... of the other team.

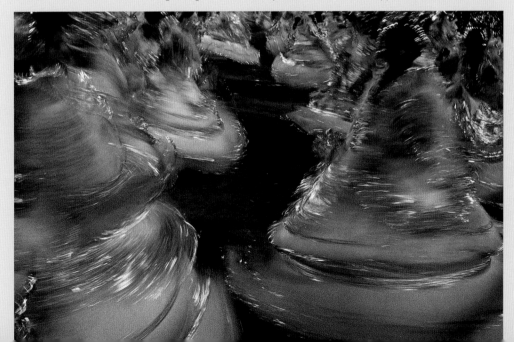

Left page: Fortaleza-CE ©R. Linsker / Rio de Janeiro-RJ ©Ed Viggiani / Following page: Fortaleza-CE ©Ed Viggiani; Fortaleza-CE ©Ed Viggiani

BRAZIL SPREADS IN ALL DIRECTIONS OVER SOUTH AMERICA. IT IN FACT COVERS ALMOST HALF THE CONTINENT, TOUCHING THE FRONTIERS OF ALL BUT TWO OF ITS THIRTEEN COUNTRIES: CHILE AND ECUADOR. IT IS HERE THAT WE HAVE OUR OWN NORTHERN HEMISPHERE (AMAZONIA, RORAIMA AND AMAPÁ) WHERE THE SEASONS ARE INVERTED IN COMPARISON WITH THE REST OF THE COUNTRY. WE ALSO HAVE A WHOLE LOT OF SOUTHERN HEMISPHERE. THE MAJOR PART OF THE COUNTRY LIES BETWEEN THE LINE OF THE EQUATOR (HEAT!) AND THE TROPIC OF CAPRICORN: YES, WE ARE TROPICAL, ALTHOUGH IN THE SOUTH WE HAVE A CERTAIN EUROPEAN AIR, WITH EVEN A LITTLE SNOW ON HIGHER GROUND.

TO THE VAST SIZE OF THE COUNTRY (MORE THAN 8 MILLION SQ. KM) IS ADDED THE DIVERSITY OF NATURE: THE WORLD OF THE AMAZON, THE COASTAL SCENERY, THE WIDE SPACES OF THE SERTÃO BACKLANDS, THE FLAT PAMPAS – AN OVERSIMPLIFICATION OF THE WORLD'S MOST BIO-DIVERSE COUNTRY. TO ENRICH THE STORY, WE SHOULD REMEMBER THAT INHABITING THE COUNTRY IS A MIXTURE OF THREE RACES – THE PORTUGUESE EUROPEAN, THE NATIVE INDIAN AND THE BLACK AFRICAN, AND THAT'S WITHOUT MENTIONING THE MILLIONS OF IMMIGRANTS THAT HAVE COME FROM ALL PARTS OF THE WORLD IN THE 20TH CENTURY. SO MANY FACTS AND FACTORS LEAD US TO ASK: IS THERE A BRAZIL? OR ARE THERE MANY BRAZILS? WE CAN ONLY ANSWER AMBIGUOUSLY: THERE IS ONE AND THERE ARE MANY. A UNIQUE AND POWERFUL TREE, WITH MANY ARMS AND MANY BRANCHES OFFERING US DIVERSE FRUITS – THE SURPRISES OFFERED US BY NATURE. SO LET US BEGIN BY PARTS, OR FROM BRANCH TO BRANCH.

Left page: Ouricuri-PE ©R. Linsker / Still photo: Gui von Schmidt

The Coast and the Atlantic Rainforest

THE EDGE OF BRAZIL: IN 1627 FRIAR VICENTE DE SALVADOR SAID THAT THE PORTUGUESE COLONISTS IN BRAZIL WERE LIKE CRABS, CLINGING TO THE BEACHES. BRAZIL CONTINUED WITH ITS FEET STUCK IN THE SAND FOR MANY DECADES, TURNING ITS BACK ON THE INTERIOR. THE COLONIZATION PROCESS HAD ITS BEGINNINGS ON THE COAST, FIRSTLY BECAUSE OF THE EASE OF COMMUNICATION WITH THE MOTHER COUNTRY, SECONDLY FOR THE GREATER ADAPTABILITY OF THE TUPI INDIANS – MASTERS OF THE COASTAL AREAS – TO THE WHITE MAN'S WAY OF LIFE. THE HISTORY OF THIS ELONGATED AND SUNNY STRIP OF BRAZIL (WITH ALMOST 8,000 KM OF BEACHES, MANGROVES AND ROCKY SHORE) MINGLES WITH THE HISTORY OF THE ATLANTIC RAINFOREST, THAT WOODED AREA BEGINNING AT THE BEACH,

CLIMBING THE SLOPES OF THE COASTAL SERRA DO MAR MOUNTAIN RANGE AND SPREADING INTO THE INTERIOR PLAINS. THE FOREST COULD BE FOUND ALONG ALMOST THE WHOLE BRAZILIAN COAST: A HISTORY OF RADICAL TRANSFORMATION. DURING THE FEW CENTURIES OF BRAZILIAN HISTORY, INDIAN FEATURES HAVE ALL BUT DISAPPEARED, WITH THE MIXED FEATURES OF BLACK AND WHITE NOW PREDOMINATING. THE TREES HAVE ALSO BEEN FELLED, BEGINNING WITH TODAY'S ALL-BUT EXTINCT BRAZILWOOD. INSTEAD, EXOTIC PLANTS (PRINCIPALLY SUGAR CANE, MANGO TREES AND COCONUT PALMS) WERE BROUGHT BY THE PORTUGUESE FROM OTHER CONTINENTS. THAT IS: EVERYTHING WE JUDGE MOST AUTHENTIC – COCONUT PALMS SWAYING IN THE BREEZE, DARK-SKINNED GIRLS IN THE SUN – WERE IN FACT IMPORTED FROM FAR AWAY.

Ilhabela-SP ©R. Linsker; Inferno beach, Rio de Janeiro-RJ ©R. Linsker

Almost
8,000 km of coast
from north to south,
holding 70%
of the Brazilian
population.

Waves of expulsion:

Saco de Mamanguá-RJ ©R. Linsker

first the Indians
were driven out,
now its the local fishermen.

KILLING THE FOREST. IN 1500 THERE WERE MORE THAN ONE MILLION SQ. KM OF FORESTED AREA ALONG THE COAST FROM RIO GRANDE DO NORTE TO RIO GRANDE DO SUL, AT TIMES HIGHER, AT TIMES DENSER, SOMETIMES REDUCED TO MANGROVE. THE NATURAL KINGDOM WAS AT ITS MOST DIVERSE IN THE ATLANTIC RAINFOREST.

EXPANSION OF AGRICULTURE, THE FELLING OF TIMBER, UNCHECKED GROWTH OF THE CITIES AND UNCONTROLLED TOURISM DESTROYED 93% OF ALL THIS NATURE UNTIL ONLY A LITTLE MORE THAN 100,000 SQ. KM REMAINS TODAY IN PARKS

AND RESERVES. EVEN SO, IN THE REMAINING SPARSE 7%, CERTAIN AREAS OF ATLANTIC RAINFOREST SHELTER THE WORLD'S GREATEST BIOLOGICAL DIVERSITY.

THE SPECIES "HOMO BRASILIENSIS" IS THAT LEAST THREATENED WITH EXTINCTION AND AT THE SAME TIME THE MOST THREATENING. THE WILDERNESS HAS LOST OUT IN THE BATTLE TO MAKE SPACE FOR SO MANY PEOPLE: MOST OF THE ANIMALS THREATENED WITH EXTINCTION IN BRAZIL ARE FROM THE ATLANTIC RAINFOREST.

INTIMATELY LINKED TO NATURE, THE INHABITANTS OF THE COAST STILL DEPEND ON CYCLES: A TIME TO FISH, A TIME TO MEND THE NETS. OVER RECENT DECADES, WITH THE ARRIVAL OF PROFESSIONAL BOATS AND PREDATORY FISHING, TIMES FOR LOCAL FISHERMEN HAVE BECOME EVER HARDER.

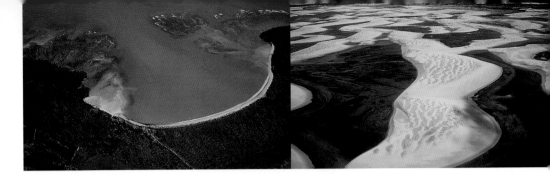

BEAUTY AND GREED. AS THE SUGAR BOOM GAVE WAY TO THAT OF GOLD AND AFTER THAT COFFEE, CATTLE AND LASTLY INDUSTRIALIZATION, THE COASTAL POPULATION WAS FORGOTTEN ON HIDDEN BEACHES, IN ISOLATED BAYS, WITH NO ROAD ACCESS, LEFT TO WREST A LIVING FROM THE SEA.

FROM PARANÁ TO RIO DE JANEIRO THEY WERE KNOWN AS CAIÇARAS AND ALONG THE COAST OF THE NORTHEAST AS JANGADEIROS (RAFT FISHERMEN). SIMILARLY TO THE INDIANS, THESE PEOPLE MADE THEIR LIVING FROM THE SEA AND FROM TINY SMALL HOLDINGS, MAKING USE OF WHAT APPEARED TO BELONG TO NO ONE. AFTER 1950, WITH THE OPENING UP OF COASTAL ROADS, LAND

SPECULATION ARRIVED TOGETHER WITH SUMMER TOURISTS. THE CITY DWELLERS ARRIVED WITH ALL THE IMPACT OF A SECOND CONQUEST: BUYING UP LAND FOR A SONG, BUILDING PRIVATE RESORTS, RAKING OVER ORCHARDS AND VEGETABLE PLOTS TO PLANT LAWNS AND PALM TREES.

"WHO EATS GRASS AND PALM TREES?" THE PERPLEXED FISHERMEN ASKED THEMSELVES.

THE PROCESS OF DISMANTLING THE LIVES OF TRADITIONAL PEOPLES SEEMS TO KNOW NO END IN BRAZIL. MEN OF THE SEA WERE DRIVEN GRADUALLY TO WALLOWING IN THE PERIPHERIES OF THE LARGE CITIES.

Comandatuba-BA ©R. Linsker; Mouth of the Jequitinhonha-BA ©R. Linsker

EIGHT THOUSAND KILOMETERS OF DIVERSITY. THE FIRST BRAZILIAN BEACHES (STARTING FROM THE NORTH) COME UNDER THE POWERFUL SWAY OF THE AMAZONIAN RIVERS, SILT-LADEN AND DARK. THEY BEGIN WITH THE RIVER OIAPO-QUE AND CONTINUE, HALF-SEA, HALF-RIVER, MOSTLY MANGROVE, UNTIL PIAUÍ AND THE DELTA OF THE RIVER PARNAÍBA.

FROM THERE TO THE GULF OF BAHIA, THE OCEAN FLOATS CRYSTAL CLEAR OVER CORAL AND SHALLOW ROCK POOLS IN LIMESTONE AND SANDSTONE REEFS WITHIN THE SEA.

THE SOUTHEAST COAST BEGINS AT THE EXTREME SOUTH OF BAHIA AND STRETCHES TO SOUTHERN SÃO PAULO STATE, BACKED, SOMETIMES NEAR, SOMETIMES FROM AFAR, BY THE COASTAL SERRA DO MAR MOUNTAIN RANGE. A STRETCH OF WIDELY DIFFERING LANDSCAPES: THE PINK CLIFFS OF SOUTHERN BAHIA DARKEN GRADUALLY INTO THE MONAZITE SAND BEACHES OF ESPIRITO SANTO, FINALLY TURNING INTO AN INDENTED COASTLINE OF INNUMERABLE BAYS AND INLETS BETWEEN RIO DE JANEIRO AND SÃO PAULO.

FROM PARANÁ SOUTHWARDS, WHAT WAS ONCE SMALL AND TUCKED AWAY IS ELONGATED INTO BEACHES AND SAND SPITS STRETCHING ALL THE WAY TO CHUÍ AT THE EXTREME SOUTHERN TIP OF BRAZIL. FULL OF TIDAL LAGOONS AND MANGROVES, THIS IS AN AREA EXTREMELY RICH IN WILDLIFE.

Fernando de Noronha N.P.-PE ©R. Linsker; Praia do Forte-BA ©R. Linsker; Abrolhos N.P.-BA ©R. Linsker

THERE IS A SPACE AND TIME IN BRAZIL WHERE LIFE PASSES CALMLY BY IN LITTLE HOUSES PAINTED IN THE MOST IMPROBABLE COLORS SUCH AS SKY BLUE AND SHOCKING PINK. THERE WHERE A SLOWLY SMOKING WOOD STOVE IS ALREADY READY TO HEAT UP A POT OF COFFEE AND THERE IS ALWAYS TIME FOR A FEW LINES OF VERSE AND THE PLAINTIVE STRUMMING OF A GUITAR AT THE END OF THE DAY. THE DAY'S BUSINESS BEGINS WELL BEFORE SUN-UP AND INVOLVES A COW WITH MILKING PROBLEMS, AN ORCHARD IN BLOOM, THE STORM THAT TOOK TILES OFF THE BARN. THEN THERE'S ALWAYS SOMEONE WHO ARRIVES TO TELL A STORY. THERE'S ALWAYS A TRANSISTOR RADIO ON THE WINDOW SILL, AND ON HEARING CERTAIN TUNES GAZES MOVE OVER THE LANDSCAPE, AND THE LISTENER UTTERS A DEEP SIGH.

THE FEEL OF THE COUNTRYSIDE

COUNTRY LIFE

Left page: Aquidauana-MS ©R. Linsker

THE PLACE CANNOT BE TOTALLY DEFINED GEOGRAPHICALLY. WE CAN BE SURE, HOWEVER, THAT IT COVERS IN SÃO PAULO STATE, SPREADS INTO MINAS GERAIS, AND INVADES A LITTLE OF GOIÁS AND MATO GROSSO. IT GOES BY THE NAME OF COUNTRYSIDE. AMBIGUOUS, THE COUNTRYSIDE OSCILLATES BETWEEN SLOW AND CALM, TRADITION AND ANACHRONISM, BUT ALWAYS POETIC.

ALTHOUGH IT REFERS TO A REGION ON THE MAP, IT ALSO SHARES SIMILARITIES WITH ALL OF THE BRAZILIAN BACKLANDS. THE SERTANEJO[1] OF THE CAATINGA[2], THE HALF-BREED OF THE AMAZON, THE COWBOY OF THE PANTANAL AND THE CAIÇARA[3] OF THE COAST ALL HAVE A LITTLE OF THE COUNTRY BOY. IN FACT, ALL OVER BRAZIL, EVEN IN THE BIG CITIES, THERE WILL ALWAYS BE THE FEEL OF THE COUNTRY. OR AT LEAST, A NOSTALGIC LONGING FOR IT

Cunha-SP ©Ed Viggiani

Translator's note: 1.Sertanejo - inhabitant of the sertão backlands. 2. Caatinga - the arid backlands of the northeast. 3. Caiçara - inhabitant of the coastal areas of the southeast.

ON BEING A COUNTRY BOY. Caipira[4] (country-boy), according to Câmara Cascudo, derives from the Indian Tupi word caapora, meaning inhabitant of the bush. There are other interpretations, including that which says caipira means shy or ashamed.

A country dweller or one intimidated by life's constraints, the Brazilian country-boy does not get upset when confronted face to face with an outsider. After all, the country-boy life is one of isolation, and a meeting, the exchange of a greeting (which can extend to a cup of coffee or a shared smoke from hand-rolled tobacco), is not an event to be let slip by:

Meetings in the countryside may not be common, but they happen. Perhaps because the country people were always located in the path of the pioneers: the Bandeirante expeditions from São Paulo setting out toward the west in search of Indian slaves in the 16th and 17th centuries; the same Paulistas that then went north to discover gold in Minas Gerais at the end of the 17th and 18th centuries; and the mule trains that for three centuries went south over the Viamão routes, looking for the bullocks that pulled the local economy. In the middle of the road, and part of all these movements, was the country-boy. Villages, small settlements, an easy life, a place for a simple rest. The countryside always represented life in transition.

Translator's note: 4. Caipira · Inhabitant of the countryside.

MANY COUNTRYSIDES. IN THIS CONSTANT PROCESS OF ADAPTATION, COUNTRY PEOPLE (PRINCIPALLY THOSE OF SÃO PAULO) GUIDED BY THE ROADS RUNNING THROUGH THEIR LANDS, BECAME MASTERS OF MIMICRY: THE COUNTRY OF THE PARAIBA VALLEY IS REMINISCENT OF RIO DE JANEIRO STATE, THE REGION AROUND THE MOGI RAILROAD REMINDS US OF MINAS GERAIS AND THE PEOPLE OF SOROCABA REMAIN UNTIL THE PRESENT DAY A BIT LIKE THE GAUCHO OF RIO GRANDE DO SUL. THESE

PAULISTA COUNTRY FOLK ADVANCED, FOLLOWING THE TRACKS OF THE PIONEERS. SLOWLY BUT SURELY, CUTTING DOWN THE FOREST, PLANTING THE CORN THAT WOULD FEED THE PIGS ON THE FARMS LEFT BEHIND, AFTERWARDS PLANTING COFFEE, THEN MOVING ON ANOTHER STEP FORWARD. SLOWLY BUT SURELY THEY OPENED UP THE STATES OF SÃO PAULO, MINAS, GOIÁS AND MATO GROSSO, BATTLING THE SAÚVA ANTS AND CUTTING DOWN ALL THE ATLANTIC RAINFOREST AROUND ABOUT.

THE COUNTRY HOUSE.

MAKING COOKIES, CHEESE BUNS, BISCUITS, CORNCAKES AND CONSERVES: ALL TO BE SOLD BY THE ROADSIDES OF MINAS. JUST AS NATURE HAS HER CYCLES, COUNTRY COOKING ALSO HAS ITS SEASONS: CHEESES ARE MADE IN THE WET SEASON DUE TO THE ABUNDANCE OF MILK; GUAVA CONSERVES IN NOVEMBER; JABUTICABA[5] JAM IN OCTOBER; IN JUNE CORN PASTE AND PANCAKES; CHEESE BUNS, CORN FLOUR AND COFFEE, IF POSSIBLE, EVERY DAY.

VISITORS ARE RECEIVED ON THE PORCH AND VERAN-DAS; THE FRONT PARLOR IS RESERVED FOR HONORED GUESTS, ON THE FEW HIGH-BACKED CHAIRS AVAILABLE; TO FRIENDS AND RELATIONS THE HEAT OF THE WOOD STOVE AND THE WIDE BEAMED WOOD-EN BENCHES IN THE KITCHEN. THOSE ARE THE RULES OF COUNTRY ETIQUETTE.

IN COUNTRY GARDENS ALL KINDS OF PLANTS ARE GROWN, ESPECIALLY IF THEY HAVE A PRETTY FLOWER. CLIMBING ROSES, DAISIES, BUSY LIZZIES, CARNATIONS (AS LONG AS THEY HAVE NOT ALREADY BEEN USED TO DECORATE A CORPSE), TREE FERNS PLANTED IN OLD COOK-ING OIL TINS; RUE TO PROTECT AGAINST THE EVIL EYE. AND THE ART OF RECYCLING: OLD CANS BECOME VASES, FLOWERS, A KID'S TOY CAR. A PIECE OF CLOTH BECOMES A CUSHION, THEN A QUILT. LUNCH BECOMES DINNER AND CASTOFF CLOTHES A FLOOR CLOTH. NOTHING IS WASTED LOST, EVERYTHING IS TRANSFORMED.

A MEASURE OF PROSE.

WORDS, EVEN IF SPOKEN SLOWLY – AFTER ALL, NOBODY MAKES HASTE – ARE SAVORED OVER SHOP COUNTERS, ON STREET CORNERS, ON SUNDAY STROLLS WHERE, IN THE TOWN SQUARE, MEN GO ROUND ONE WAY AND WOMEN THE OTHER, SO THAT GLANCES CAN BE INTERCEPTED MORE EASILY.

IN THE COUNTRY THERE'S TIME TO CON-VERSE OVER LUNCH, AT SUNDOWN AND AT NIGHTFALL. BUT NOT IN THE MORNING: DAILY TOIL STARTS EARLY IN THE COUNTRY.

5. Jabuticaba - small berry used to make conserves.

Previous page: Serra da Mantiqueira-SP ©R. Linsker / Diamantina-MG ©Miguel Aun

PANTANAL

BRAZIL HAS ALWAYS LOOKED TO THE SEA, AND (UNTIL RECENTLY) VERY LITTLE TO AN INLAND FRESHWATER SEA, ONE OF THE WORLD'S RICHEST WILDLIFE AREAS. DUE TO ITS LOCATION AT THE WESTERN EDGES OF BRAZIL, ALMOST PENETRATING BOLIVIA AND FLOODED FOR A GOOD PART OF THE YEAR, IT REMAINED ISOLATED FOR A CENTURY AND A HALF. THIS HAS BEEN FOR THE GOOD. IT'S WELL KNOWN THAT IN BRAZIL AMNESIA HAS ALWAYS BEEN THE BEST CONSERVATIONIST.

Aquidauana-MS ©V. Cunha

A TRUE AFFIRMATION, BUT IN THIS CASE UNFAIR: THE GREAT PRESERVER OF THE PANTANAL – ONE OF THE MOST VALUABLE PIECES OF BRAZIL'S NATURAL HERITAGE – WAS ALWAYS THE INHABITANT OF THE PANTANAL. WHETHER RANCHER OR RANCH HAND, HE NEVER ATTEMPTED TO CHANGE THE COURSE OF NATURE, ALTER RIVERS OR DRAIN THE WETLANDS, IN SHORT, DESTROY NATURE.

MEN TIRED OF STRUGGLING IN THE MINES OF CORUMBÁ, WHERE THE LAND ALREADY HAD NOTHING MORE TO OFFER, AND WHO HAD MOVED INTO THE PANTANAL TWO HUNDRED YEARS BEFORE, REALIZED THEY HAD TO SIMPLY ACCEPT WHAT LOCAL NATURE HAD TO OFFER. THIS WAS NOT A PITTANCE: THERE WAS PASTURE IDEAL FOR EXTENSIVE CATTLE RANCHING, PLENTIFUL WATER AS LONG AS THE WET/DRY

Pantanal Deer ©V. Cunha; *"Theristicus cauditus"* ©V. Cunha

CYCLE WAS RESPECTED. THERE WAS A BROADNESS TO THE LANDSCAPE, A HORIZON SO WIDE THAT WHAT COULD HAVE APPEARED AS A LIMITATION – THE ANNUAL FLOOD CYCLE – SEEMED MORE LIKE FREEDOM IN AN INFINITE SKY. A NATURAL DEPRESSION IN THE MIDDLE OF SOUTH AMERICA RESULTING FROM THE EMERGENCE OF THE ANDES, RARELY RISING MORE THAN 100 METERS ABOVE SEA LEVEL, THE LOW-LYING PLAIN OF THE PANTANAL IS FLOODED ANNUALLY BY THE RIVERS OF THE PARAGUAY WATER BASIN. IN THE WET SEASON UP TO TWO-THIRDS OF ITS 180,000 SQ. KM LIES UNDERWATER. MAN AND BEAST THEN HAVE TO SEEK SHELTER WHEREVER THEY CAN FIND IT.

A ROUND-UP OF THE WILDLIFE. THE WIDE HORIZONS, THE LACK OF HEIGHTS OR NATURAL IMPEDIMENTS MAKES THE PANTANAL PERFECT FOR THE OBSERVATION OF ANIMAL LIFE. THE REGION IS HOME TO OVER SIX HUNDRED SPECIES OF BIRDS, EIGHTY SPECIES OF MAMMALS, TWO HUNDRED AND SIXTY OF FISH AND FIFTY REPTILES. NUMBERS ARE INCREASING, EXCEPT THOSE OF THE JAGUAR, MERCILESSLY HUNTED IN THE PAST BY RANCHERS WHO SAW IT AS A THREAT TO THEIR CATTLE. IN THE BIRD-BREEDING SEASON IN SEPTEMBER, NESTLINGS MAKE A SYMPHONY OF CALLS THAT RESOUND OVER THE PLAINS.

THE HUGE VARIETY OF FRESHWATER FISH PRESENTS AN EVER-GROWING ATTRACTION TO SPORTS FISHERMEN. THE SOUTH AMERICAN ALLIGATOR OR CAYMAN, ALMOST HUNTED TO EXTINCTION FOR ITS SKIN IN THE EIGHTIES, HAS MADE A COME-BACK IN THE RIVERS AND LAGOONS. IT IS ESTIMATED THAT THERE ARE 600,000 CAPYBARA (A RODENT THE SIZE OF A PIG), 35,000 DEER AND A SIMILAR NUMBER OF BUCK IN THE PANTANAL. NOT TO MENTION SNAKES, LIZARDS, AND OTHER SMALLER ANIMALS SUCH AS THE COATI, SOUTH AMERICAN COUSIN TO THE RACCOON. HUMANS ARE IN THE MINORITY.

PROBLEMS COME FROM OUTSIDE. THE GREATEST VILLAINS IN THE PANTANAL LIVE ON ITS BORDERS IN THE FORM OF IRRESPONSIBLE FARMERS THAT DESTROY THE FORESTS, SILT THE RIVERS AND POLLUTE THE WATERS WITH FERTILIZER AND PESTICIDE. REGIONS SUCH AS THAT OF THE RIVER TAQUARAL NO LONGER SERVE AS DRAINAGE CHANNELS IN

THE WET CYCLE DUE TO THE LEVEL OF SILTING. MANY FORMERLY PRODUCTIVE RANCHES NOW LIE UNDERWATER. GOLD DIGGERS IN POCONÉ HAVE POLLUTED THE WATERS WITH MERCURY, THE LEVEL OF RESULTANT DAMAGE STILL UNKNOWN. PREDATORY FISHING IN THE RIVER PARAGUAY HAS LED TO A REDUCTION IN THE NUMBER OF FISH IN THE REGION'S RIVERS. HOWEVER, NOTHING THREATENED THE PANTANAL SO MUCH AS PLANS MADE IN 1989 TO TURN THE RIVER PARAGUAY INTO A CANALIZED WATERWAY, STRAIGHTENING ITS BENDS AND ALTERING THE WHOLE SYSTEM OF FLOODING AND DRAINAGE IN THE PANTANAL. ENVIRONMENTAL PRESSURE GROUPS SUCCESSFULLY BLOCKED THE PLAN.

LAND OF THE PEÃO. THE AMBITION OF THE INHABITANT OF THE PANTANAL, THE PEÃO, ACCORDING TO WRITER ABÍLIO LEITE DE BARROS, WAS TO HAVE "A GOOD HORSE, WELL-SADDLED, AND A WOMAN – IN THAT ORDER". APART FROM SIMPLE DREAMS, DAILY ROUTINE BEGINS BEFORE DAWN, WORKING WITH THE CATTLE, AND ENDS WITH A CIRCLE PARTAKING OF TERERÊ (A LEGACY OF THE CHIMARRÃO TEA OF THE GAUCHOS, SERVED ICE COLD DUE TO THE EXCESSIVE HEAT), WHETTING THE APPETITE FOR A GOOD CHAT. FROM ONE DAY TO THE NEXT, ONE CHALLENGE AFTER ANOTHER, THE PEÃO IS ALWAYS ARMED WITH A KNIFE AND GUN AT HIS BELT, READY TO FACE THE WILDLIFE THAT'S NEVER FAR FROM THE DOOR: JAGUARS, ANACONDAS, WILD PIGS, POISONOUS SNAKES AND MORE.

BONITO. NEARBY, NEIGHBORING MIRANDA BUT OUTSIDE THE PANTANAL PROPER, IS THE TOWN OF BONITO. THE SEAFLOOR DURING THE PALEOZOIC ERA, TODAY'S LIMESTONE LANDSCAPES ARE HOME TO CRYSTAL-CLEAR STREAMS AND RIVERS. SWIMMING IN THEIR WATERS IS LIKE FLOATING IN PARADISE, SURROUNDED BY ENCHANTED GARDENS OF AQUATIC PLANTS AND BALLERINAS, A DREAM WORLD UNIQUE TO BONITO.

Preservation through poverty: many of the country's colonial cities and monuments are today applauding the fact that progress passed them by when economic activity suddenly changed direction. In this shortsighted 20th century, many Brazilian towns have had their architectural past destroyed in favor of high-rise buildings; old houses and monuments in favor of factories; wooden walls exchanged for aluminum siding; their beauty and tradition for soulless ugliness.

Colonial Cities.

THE BEAUTY OF OUR PAST.

The wealth of old economies generated what we today call our Historical Heritage. On the sea coast – Salvador(BA), Olinda(PE), São Luís(MA), Parnaiba(PI), João Pessoa(PB) and others – were built on the wealth provided by sugar cane and enslaved labor (1580 to 1700). In the interior of Brazil – the historic cities of Minas, Goiás and Bahia – were built in the following boom cycle (1700 to 1808), with the discovery of gold and diamonds.

At the height of the colonial period, power was embodied in the church and the state. And it was the architecture that left no one in doubt as to who was giving the orders.

The principal colonial cities in Brazil were built on a triangular power base: civil, military and religious. Government palaces, chambers of commerce

and prisons revealed the mother country's power; the castles and fortifications that of the military; while the power of religion was shown in churches, convents, monasteries and colleges. Salvador, for example, has 365 churches. And in order to capture the faithful, the best of the epoch's wealth in gold and art was offered:

WORLD HERITAGE SITES. *Ouro Preto (MG), on the previous page and São Luís (MA), have been declared World Heritage Sites by UNESCO due to their architectural heritage.*

São Luís is the daughter of sugar cane and still shows in the facades of its houses the Moorish influence of the famous Portuguese tiles. The city was named in honor of Louis XIII during the French invasion of the northeast (1612 to 1615). The French heritage has disappeared.

Ouro Preto was born of gold fever, after the Paulista bandeirante Antônio Dias de Oliveira found deposits close to the Itacolomi Peak (1700). Within 12 years, virtually all able-bodied men in both the colony and in Portugal had made for the mines. Lisbon was left empty.

And if, at the beginning, haste to extract the gold took precedence over building fine houses, over succeeding decades attention returned to architecture. The inhabitants of Minas Gerais hotly disputed who had the most beautiful house or the richest church.

BAROQUE BRAZIL. *From 1580 to 1640 Portugal suffered under the thumb of Spanish kings. With the help of England the empire was regained, this time with Brazil at its epicenter. Luck and fate: the gold of Minas Gerais allows for refinement and luxury, of which baroque is the maximum expression.*

"As opposed to Renaissance architecture, focussed on the intellect, the baroque resides in the imagination*"

With its exuberant tropical nature, the country already naturally excited the imagination with its forests, smells and colors. In this paradise of the senses, the Portuguese Baroque was perfected and became Brazilian Baroque, the first cultural manifestation that could really be called our own.

The maximum expression of this baroque occurred in Minas Gerais, through the talents of painters such as Manuel da Costa Ataíde, Bernardo Pires and João Soares de Araújo and the sculptor and architect Antônio Francisco Lisboa, the "little cripple".

And it is perhaps because of this refined birth certificate that we are so baroque today, a people prone to an exaggerated touching of the forelock and attention to detail.

*Nicolau Sevcenko, in O Universo Mágico do Barroco Brasileiro

Out of the total heritage of Brazilian colonial history, IPHAN (The National Institute for Historical and Artistic History) has:

- *Put preservation orders on over 16,000 buildings, as well as*
- *Fifty colonial urban centers*

UNESCO has declared nine cultural and natural monuments in Brazil to be World Heritage Sites:

- *The architectural and urban complex of Ouro Preto / MG*
- *The colonial center of Olinda / PE*
- *Historical and archeological sites of the Jesuit missions to the Guarani Indians / RS*
- *The colonial center of Salvador / BA*
- *The Bom Jesus de Matosinhos Sanctuary / MG*
- *Architectural and urban complex of São Luís / MA*

AMA ZÔ NIA

MANY-MYTHED AMAZON. THE AMAZON WAS BORN STIGMATIZED BY MYTH, BEGINNING WITH THE NAME. IN 1542, FRANCISCO DE ORELLANA, THE MONK GUSTAVO DE CARVAJAL AND A HANDFUL OF OTHERS RETURNED TO SPAIN AFTER DESCENDING THE HUGE RIVER BY CANOE. THEY JUSTIFIED ABANDONING THEIR LEADER GONÇALO BY THE FACT THAT THEY WERE UNABLE TO UPSTREAM AGAINST THE RIVER'S CURRENT AND ALSO THAT THEY WERE ATTACKED BY FEMALE WARRIORS. THE REGION THUS BECAME FAMOUS IN EUROPE AS THE "LAND OF THE AMAZONS", AFTER THE ANCIENT GREEK MYTH.

Left page: Amapá ©L. McIntyre

133

THE ECOLOGICAL IMPORTANCE OF THE FOREST. IN 1971, DUE TO AN ERROR MADE BY A JOURNALIST WORKING FOR AN AMERICAN AGENCY, THE IDEA TOOK ROOT THAT THE AMAZON WORKED AS THE LUNGS OF THE WORLD, DUE TO ITS ENORMOUS CAPACITY TO SYNTHESIZE OXYGEN. IN FACT, HARALD SIOLI, THE GERMAN SCIENTIST FROM THE MAX PLANCK INSTITUTE WHO GAVE THE INTERVIEW, MENTIONED CO_2 RATHER THAN O_2 AS HAD BEEN ᴺ ᴮᵞ ᵀᴴᴱ JOURNALIST. SCIENTISTS AGREE ⸏⸏ LARGᴱ

For some centuries the Amazon was seen as a potential earthly paradise or else as the location of mythical countries, kingdoms of untold wealth such as Eldorado, a city whose king bathed himself in gold, or La Canela, the spice kingdom.

With the passing of centuries, and with the difficulties encountered in attempting its settlement — for example such unsuccessful undertakings as the construction of the Madeira-Mamoré railway in which thousands of people died — it became redefined as the "Green Hell".

It is in fact neither hell nor paradise, but in fact the last, vast tract of untouched tropical forest in the world, a gigantic area of five and a half million km², 60% of which within Brazilian territory.

And if the world is really heading for serious problems in its supply of fresh water, as seems likely, the Amazon will definitely qualify as a paradise. The basin of the Amazon River alone, covering an area of six million km², pours the equivalent of 20% of the world's Ocean.

the equivale...
rivers into the Atlantic Oc...
Another myth to be debunked is that the Amazon is an uninhabited wilderness, devoid of people. The great forest has received most attention for its flora, animals and Indians, today reduced to a fraction of their original population. This is highly unfair to the caboclo, that mixture of Indian and white who lives in harmony with the environment despite the difficulties in making a living, where from apparent abundance little can really be used.

The caboclo is the reason that the forest is still standing and he can teach us much about its management, including medicinal plants and life in the Amazon in general. Conservation will only work if we learn the lesson the caboclo has to teach.

WRITTEN BY THE ~~~~ ~~~~ ~~~~ TODAY THAT THE AMAZON, AS ALL ~~~ ~~ FORESTS, HAS A GIGANTIC CAPACITY TO EXTRACT FROM THE ATMOSPHERE THE CO_2 PRODUCED BY THE LARGE-

SCALE BURNING OF FOSSIL FUELS SUCH AS GAS, COAL AND OIL, RETURNING IT TO THE RIVERS AND SOIL. RATHER THAN THE WORLD'S LUNG, AS LUIZ CARLOS MOLION OF THE INPE (NATIONAL INSTITUTE OF SPACE RESEARCH) EXPLAINS, THE AMAZON IS IN FACT THE FILTER OF THE WORLD.

MAN PUTS 5 BILLION TONS OF CARBON INTO THE ATMOSPHERE PER ANNUM. ACCORDING TO THESE CALCULATIONS, THE AMAZON EXTRACTS 1.2 BILLION TONS OF CARBON PER ANNUM, AND IN SO DOING SOLVES ONE-FIFTH OF THE PROBLEM.

Chameleon ©L. Principe; Sloths, *Bradypus trydactilus* ©L. Principe

NEW THEORIES, HOWEVER, AFFIRM THAT ITS IMPORTANCE IS NOT RESTRICTED TO THIS. THE AMAZON, WITH ITS ENORMOUS TRANSPIRATION AND EVAPORATION FROM THE TREES, FEEDS HEAT TO THE UPPER LAYERS OF THE ATMOSPHERE AND THEREBY RAISES TEMPERATURES IN THE NORTHERN HEMISPHERE. IF THERE WERE NO FOREST, THEREFORE, WINTERS IN THE NORTHERN HEMISPHERE WOULD BE LONGER AND MUCH COLDER.

THE AMAZON WITHOUT TREES: A DESERT. FERTILE SOILS DO EXIST IN THE AMAZON, FOR EXAMPLE IN THE STATE OF ACRE. BUT THE TRUTH IS THAT THE GREAT MAJORITY OF SOILS IN THE WORLD'S GREATEST FOREST ARE EXTREMELY POOR, OLD, AND STRIPPED OF THEIR NUTRIENTS BY THE SEAS AND RIVERS OF

SUCCESSIVE GEOLOGICAL ERAS. SCIENTISTS STATE WITH WONDER THAT THE AMAZON IN FACT LIVES OFF ITSELF, FROM THE ORGANIC MATERIAL THAT IT PRODUCES. FOR THIS REASON THE SPEED OF THE FOLIAGE AND DECOMPOSITION CYCLES.

THE HIGH DEGREE OF DIVERSITY IN ITS PLANT SPECIES IS THEREFORE NECESSARY FOR SURVIVAL: EACH TREE HAS ITS OWN METHOD OF PUTTING DOWN ROOTS AND ABSORBING NUTRIENTS, THEREBY MAKING MAXIMUM USE OF THE SCARCE RESOURCES AVAILABLE. THESE LOW NUTRITIONAL LEVELS OF THE VEGETABLE WORLD CAN SUPPORT ONLY A LESS RICH ANIMAL LIFE AND, CONSEQUENTLY, A LESS ABUNDANT LIFE FOR MAN.

THE FOREST IS STILL A MYSTERY IN TERMS OF ITS SHARE OF THE PLANET'S BIO-DIVERSITY. SOME RESEARCHERS, HOWEVER, ESTIMATE THAT 30% OF THE WORLD'S GENETIC DATABASE RESIDES IN THE AMAZON.

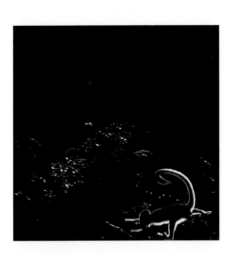

Left page: Jarilândia-PA ©L. McIntyre / Squirrel monkey ©P. Martinelli; Wooly monkey. *Lagothrix lagothricha* ©L. Príncipe

Rio Negro-AM ©L. Principe

CHICO MENDES. CHICO MENDES WAS A LUCKY BOY, OR PERHAPS EXTREMELY UNLUCKY. MAYBE BETTER THAN BOTH, HE WAS A MAN MARKED BY FATE. HE COULD HAVE CARRIED ON RUBBER TAPPING, SEMI-LITERATE, CERTAINLY SIDELINED, BUT LIFE DECIDED TO PUT HIM AT THE CENTER OF THE STORM. IN THE RUBBER RESERVE OF HIS YOUTH, HE WAS TAUGHT BY EUCLIDES TÁVORA, A COUSIN OF JUAREZ TÁVORA, A FIGHTER WHO WAS HIDING IN THE FOREST TO ESCAPE POLITICAL PERSECUTION. THIS MEETING INDELIBLY STAMPED CHICO'S SHORT LIFE. CHICO GREW UP AND INVOLVED HIMSELF IN THE RUBBER TAPPERS' STRUGGLE AND ACHIEVED WORLD RENOWN. HE WAS ONE OF THOSE WHO ALTER THE COURSE OF HISTORY. THE WORLD CAME TO REALIZE THAT THE DESCENDANTS OF THE RUBBER TAPPERS OF THE TURN OF THE CENTURY WERE STILL LIVING IN THE FOREST, AND THE GROTESQUE SUFFERING TO WHICH THEIR LIVES WERE SUBJECTED WAS REVEALED. BUT HE ACHIEVED MUCH MORE THAN THIS: HE STOPPED THE CHAINSAWS, BLOCKED THE CONSTRUCTION OF ABSURD ROADS WITH A PEACEFUL TECHNIQUE CALLED "STAND-OFFS". HOWEVER, HE DID NOT RECEIVE THE PROTECTION HE DESERVED AND WAS EXECUTED BY RANCHERS. AFTER HIS DEATH, THE RUBBER TAPPERS SUCCEEDED IN GETTING THEIR EXTRACTIVE RESERVES DEMARCATED, THE ANNUAL BURN-OFFS IN THE AMAZON DIMINISHED, AND THE ENVIRONMENTAL QUESTION GAINED NATIONAL IMPORTANCE IN BRAZIL. IT IS LEFT FOR US TO GIVE THANKS FOR HIS SACRIFICE, THE SACRED LABOR OF CHICO MENDES.

THE TRIBES. EVIDENCE EXISTS THAT AROUND 1500 THERE WERE LARGE TRIBES SPREAD ALONG THE AMAZON RIVER, LIVING IN EXTENSIVE WELL-ORGANIZED INDIGENOUS COMMUNITIES. THE MEETING WITH THE WHITE MAN WAS FATAL FOR THESE PEOPLE. AROUND 1720, A REBELLION LED BY THE INDIGENOUS CHIEF AJURICABA IN THE UPPER NEGRO RIVER REGION WAS ABLE TO HOLD OFF THE EXPANSION OF THE PORTUGUESE FOR MANY YEARS.

IN 1845, WITH THE GREAT DROUGHT IN THE NORTHEAST AND THE DEVELOPMENT OF RUBBER TAPPING IN THE AMAZON, A NEW WAVE OF MIGRANTS ARRIVED IN THE REGION, CAUSING FURTHER CONFLICT WITH THE INDIANS AND THE DISAPPEARANCE OF MORE TRIBES.

HUNDREDS OF THOUSANDS OF PEOPLE FROM THE DROUGHT-STRICKEN NORTHEAST SET OFF FOR THE LAND OF WATERS TO REBUILD THEIR LIVES. THE CABOCLO (MEANING COPPER-COLORED) AROSE FROM THE MIXTURE OF NORTHEASTERNERS WITH INDIANS*.

THE DECLINE OF THE RUBBER BOOM IN A WAY "SAVED" THE LIVES OF MANY TRIBES, GIVEN THAT THE INDIANS' WORST ENEMIES AT THE BEGINNING OF THE CENTURY WERE THE RUBBER TAPPERS AND THE LANDOWNERS. WITH THE COLLAPSE OF THE RUBBER INDUSTRY, THE INDIANS WERE GIVEN A BRIEF RESPITE UNTIL THE OPENING UP OF ROADS IN THE AMAZON REGION IN THE SEVENTIES.

Left page: Parintins-AM ©L. Principe / Macaws, Marajó-PA ©R. Faquini

* Câmara Cascudo, *Dicionário do Folclore Brasileiro*

Heights:
Sierras, Mountains
and Plateaus

Brazil, geology tells us, is an ancient land. Stable. To put it simply, this means that the Brazilian shield upon which we rest no longer yearns for the excitement of youth or any extreme movement, whether upwards or to the side. Geologically speaking, the country can be likened to a comfortably retired gentleman. Seventy million years have passed since the last major seismic transformation. That was when the volcanic island of Fernando de Noronha rose from the sea and the Itatiaia Massif was extruded between Rio de Janeiro and São Paulo. For those who feel that extruded is a rather violent word, try imagining the scene: an entire mountain, emerging from the center of the earth in one cataclysmic upheaval. This long period of stability has resulted not in high mountains but in escarpments and plateaus. These began to appear around 250 million years ago, when the world's land mass, joined together in one continent called Pangea, split in two along an east-west axis. This abrupt movement caused a huge bubble to rise in the interior of Brazil. The heights that remained corresponded to the land that did not settle, neither succumbed to the erosion of rain, wind and time. Our mountains and plateaus are above all resistant.

Myths and
mountains
go together.
Macunaíma,
a playful indigenous
god, is supposed
to have been born
on Mount Roraima
(RR) (2,772 m).
Below him,
on the savannas of
Roraima, the land
of Eldorado was
supposed to exist,
where the king
bathed himself
daily in gold.
On Neblina Peak
(AM), Brazil's
highest at 3,014 m,
gold is not a myth
and the inhospitable
environment is
frequented almost
only by Ianomâni
Indians and gold
prospectors.

Serra do Padre range, near Neblina Peak-AM ©L. Principe

THE CHAPADA DIAMANTINA PLATEAU (BA). In the middle of the state of Bahia an island of considerable heights (1700m) blocks the passage of clouds that would otherwise bring rain to the sertão. A green oasis that delights tourists: the Chapada Diamantina Plateau. In the 19th century, diamond and gold fever brought prospectors to the Serra do Sincorá

mountain range and its surroundings. Fine cities sprang up, some of them now in ruins mysteriously decorating the byways. Today, nature in the Diamantina Plateau with its rivers, caverns and colonial cities attracts a different kind of prospector: those looking for beautiful scenery.

Chapada dos Guimarães N.P.-MT ©Ed Viggiani; Chapada Diamantina N.P.-BA ©R. Linsker

THE CHAPADA DOS GUIMARÃES (MS). The geodesic center of South America is located in the middle of this beautiful set of orange-colored mountains, discovered around 1718, when the Paulista bandeirante expeditions, virtually expelled by the Portuguese from recently discovered Minas Gerais, came in search of gold. There was gold in Cuiabá (MS), but this soon became worked out and the region forgotten until

the 1960s, when it was reached by the advancing agricultural frontier. Its waters and waterfalls, the heights of the Chapada (on average 800m) and its more amenable temperatures – when compared to the scalding heat of Cuiabá – have made the region an increasingly attractive destination for tourists. They say it's the magnetism of the geodesic center...

The land of Brazil

has been sculpted from
north to south by the forces

Serra da Capivara N.P.-PI ©R. Linsker

of water,
   time and the wind.

Sete Cidades N.P.-PI ©L. McIntyre; Pico das Almas-BA ©R. Linsker

THE MOUNTAINS AND THE SEA.

Between 180 and 70 million years ago, the southern continent, called Gondwana, also split into the continents of South America and Africa. Two important mountain ranges were formed from this rupture. One remains below the ocean, the Mid-Atlantic Ridge, rising to enormous heights. On the Brazilian side rose the spinal column of the Serra do Mar and Mantiqueira ranges, sufficiently high to prevent the Atlantic rain clouds from reaching beyond, so that rain always falls along the entire range. This configuration allowed the formation of one of the most beautiful and diverse forests on earth, the Atlantic Rainforest, the most Brazilian of ecosystems, as it penetrates only slightly into other countries of South America.

Serra dos Órgãos N.P.-RJ ©R. Linsker

GAUCHOS, PAMPAS AND MATE TEA.

AROUND THE YEAR 1620 THERE WAS NO DOUBT THAT, ACCORDING TO THE TREATY OF TORDESILLAS, THE PROVINCE OF RIO GRANDE DO SUL BELONGED TO SPAIN. HOWEVER THE TEMPTATION WAS TOO GREAT FOR THE BANDEIRANTE INDIAN HUNTERS FROM SÃO PAULO. AND THERE WERE MANY INDIAN BRAVES QUARTERED IN THE SPANISH JESUIT MISSIONS IN THE AREA NOW COMPRISING THE STATES OF PARANÁ, SANTA CATARINA AND RIO GRANDE DO SUL. EVEN BETTER, THEY WERE EASY PREY, DOCILE AND UNARMED.

HISTORIANS NOWADAYS QUESTION WHETHER THERE EVER WAS ANY LARGE SCALE BANDEIRANTE WAR AGAINST THE MISSIONS, AS THE JESUITS AND THE SPANISH CLAIM, OR WHETHER THE INDIANS SIMPLY ABANDONED THE VILLAGES TO REGAIN A LITTLE OF THEIR FREEDOM WITH THE HALF-BREED PAULISTAS. THE FACT IS THAT FROM THIS PAULISTA TERRITORIAL INVASION, FROM THIS FUSION OR CONFUSION, WAS BORN THE GAUCHO: HALF-SPANISH, HALF-PORTUGUESE, AND MAINLY INDIAN.

ONE OF THE MOST CHARACTERISTIC CUSTOMS OF RIO GRANDE DO SUL, THE DRINKING OF ERVA MATE, OR CHIMARRÃO, WAS AN INDIAN LEGACY THAT THE MISSION JESUITS WERE UNABLE TO ERADICATE. PONCHOS, THE OPEN CAMPFIRE, THE USE OF THE BOLEADA TO CAPTURE CATTLE, THE LOVE OF AN OPEN LIFE ON THE PLAINS, ALL THIS CAME FROM THE INDIGENOUS PEOPLE, AND WAS AS STRONG IN THE REGION AS THE MINUANO WIND.

UNTIL THE 19TH CENTURY, GAUCHO WAS A RATHER DEROGATORY TERM FOR A BRAVE, FAST-TALKING, SOMETIME CATTLE RUSTLER. WITH THE PASSAGE OF TIME, THE QUALITY THAT STOOD OUT WAS BRAVERY, AND TRADITION DID THE REST. THE GAUCHO HAS BECOME THE SYMBOL OF A DEEPLY ROOTED PEOPLE, FAITHFUL TO THEIR CULTURE, ABLE TO FLY OVER THE PAMPAS ON THE BACK OF THEIR STURDY MOUNTS.

REGIONAL IDENTITY. FROM 1835 TO 1845 RIO GRANDE DO SUL WAS TORN APART IN A BLOODY REBELLION AGAINST THE SECOND BRAZILIAN EMPIRE. BENTO GONÇALVEZ, LEADER OF THE LOCAL CAUDILHOS, PROCLAIMED THE RIO GRANDENSE OR PIRATINI REPUBLIC IN THE STATE AND IN 1839 THE ITALIAN REVOLUTIONARY GIUSEPPE GARIBALDI AND DAVI CANABARRO EXTENDED THE REVOLUTION TO SANTA CATARINA, PROCLAIMING THE CATARINENSE OR JULIAN REPUBLIC. FOR THE FIRST TIME IN BRAZIL, A STRONG FEELING OF REGIONAL IDENTITY WAS BORN. IN THE WAR OF THE RAGGED (FARRAPOS), AS IT WAS CALLED, THE REPUBLIC WAS FINALLY DEFEATED IN 1845 BY THE DUKE OF CAXIAS, BUT NOT BEFORE ESTABLISHING THE PRIDE OF THE GAUCHO FOR HIS LAND AND HIS STRUGGLE, A SENTIMENT THAT HAS CONTINUED UNTIL TODAY.

Left page: Southern frontier, Bagé-RS ©L. Plentz

MY KINGDOM FOR A HORSE. THE DESTRUCTION OF THE MISSIONS LEFT HERDS OF CATTLE TO ROAM WILD AND MULTIPLY UNTIL THE FOLLOWING CENTURY AND THE DISCOVERY OF GOLD IN MINAS GERAIS. THE VIAMÃO TRAIL WAS THEN OPENED UP FROM SOROCABA IN SÃO PAULO STATE TO THE PAMPAS OF RIO GRANDE DO SUL, TAKING BULLOCKS, MULES AND HORSES FROM THE SOUTH TO THE MINES IN MINAS. IT WAS THROUGH THIS TRADE THAT PORTUGAL WAS ABLE ANNEX THE SOUTHERN LANDS TO ITS BRAZILIAN EMPIRE ONCE AND FOR ALL.

SETTLEMENT OF GAUCHO TERRITORY BEGAN IN 1737 WITH THE FOUNDATION OF RIO GRANDE DE SÃO PEDRO, BECOMING DEFINITIVE IN THE YEARS BETWEEN 1770 AND 1801. MAN AND HORSE WON THE PLAINS AND THE CAMPAIGNS, FOUNDED SIX HUNDRED VAST RANCHES, WHERE THERE WAS HARDLY ANY SLAVE LABOR BUT RATHER WAGE EARNERS. THE HALF-BREED BRAVE SKILLED AT TRANSFORMING AN UNTAMED HORSE INTO A FLEET, ELEGANT MOUNT, THE MAN WITH THE CHIMARRÃO, WAS THE HERO OF THIS EPIC STORY. CATTLE RAISING ON THE RANCHES OF THE INTERIOR AND THE PROCESSING OF BEEF INTO JERKY BECAME THE REGION'S PRINCIPAL ECONOMIC ACTIVITIES.

JESUITS. WITH THEIR GREAT TALENT FOR LEADERSHIP AND ORGANIZA-
TION, THE JESUITS SUFFERED NUMEROUS SETBACKS IN THE COLONIAL
PERIOD, BOTH DURING THAT OF PORTUGAL AND OF SPAIN.
AT THE BEGINNING, THESE QUALITIES WERE WIDELY USED BY THE
SPANISH KINGS WHO FELT THAT THEY COULD ONLY GUARANTEE
CONTROL OF THE REGION THROUGH THE JESUIT SETTLEMENTS.

São Miguel das Missões-RS ©L. Plentz

WITH THE FIVE SUCCESSIVE PAULISTA ATTACKS THAT OCCURRED BETWEEN 1635 AND 1638, THE JESUITS LOST OVER THIRTEEN MISSIONS, HANGING ON ONLY TO THE SEVEN PEOPLES OF THE MISSIONS. THE INDIANS CONTINUED TO BE CONVERTED BY THE JESUITS UNTIL THE LATTER'S EXPULSION FROM BRAZIL BY THE MARQUIS OF POMBAL IN 1759.

Sertão: Cerrado Caatinga

The Sertão: the land inside.

The sertão was the interior, everything that was inside, out of eyesight of the people living on the coast. That was how Pero Vaz de Caminha alluded to it, and later Father Antônio Vieira and so many other writers afterwards.

Câmara Cascudo also mentioned that the word sertão could be a contraction of "desertão", signifying big desert in Portuguese, which only confirms the impression of isolation evoked by the word; as if the inside was, in fact, the end of the world.

Even the latest revision of the country's constitution forgets our sertão: the cerrado and the caatinga, its principal ecosystems, are not given national heritage status, while the Amazon, the Atlantic Rainforest and the Pantanal wetlands are; environmental favoritism?

In practice this neglect has been fatal to the two ecosystems. The caatinga in the country's northeast (around 800,000 km²), apparently a strong, aggressive survivor, is so fragile as to be unable to recover in soil that has been ploughed over or cultivated. It is estimated that in the "last fifteen years, 40,000 km² of this ecosystem have been transformed into a desert due to man's interference in the region's environment" (WWF).

The two million km² of cerrado in the center-west of the country have, by the same token, also undergone radical change. It is estimated that by the turn of the millennium over 70% of its original area will have been irrevocably altered. It is the second most degraded ecosystem in the country, behind only the Atlantic Rainforest, now down to the last remaining 7%.

Left page: Itambé Massif - Diamantina-MG ©R. Linsker / Barbalha - Chapada do Araripe-CE ©R. Linsker

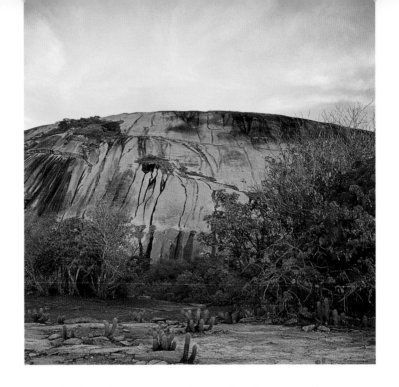

The Sertão that is Cerrado.
The cerrado is a land of extremes:
the second greatest vegetation zone in Brazil
and currently the most devastated and
also that which contains the least number
of protected areas (only 2% of its extent).

At first, in colonial times, mining was the
greatest villain, sullying the water and silting
the rivers. In the 1950s, with the march
to the west, this vast area, considered "useless"
until then, was opened up for extensive
cattle ranching and one-crop cultivation,
mainly soybeans.

CATTLE AND DESTINY.

The sertões live and die from the same things: one-crop agriculture and cattle. Cotton in the caatinga, soybeans in the cerrado.

In the northeast, the so-called leather culture began at the end of the 17th century and went on into the 18th and 19th centuries, supplying Brazil with jerked beef. The cattle multiplied and the cowboys penetrated further into the sertão, displacing Indians and expanding the ranches.

This culture of the cowboy continues to the present day. The brave and skillful man, clothed from head to foot in the leather that allows him to ride through the thorny scrub. In Brazil's center-west, it was again cattle that opened up the territory. Multiplying on their own, the herds required only two or three ranch hands to look after a thousand head. Rodeos are symbolic of this Brazilian interior: a virile demonstration of the cowboy's skills on horseback.

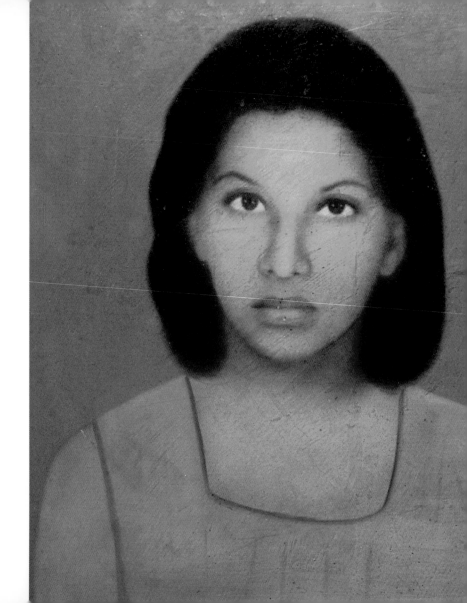

Clouds often remain stationary over the sertão, without

releasing a drop of rain.
An agony of waiting.
They neither drop their load
nor move on.

The Sertão that is Caatinga.
"From January onwards,
the inhabitant of the sertão
gazes at the horizon for
hours on end, like a madman
inside a burning house".*
Twenty million Brazilians
live, if not constantly looking
at the sky, then in constant
fear of drought. For this has
been the sad cycle of life
in the sertão, one of the
country's first regions to be
settled, and one of the world's
most heavily populated
semi-arid regions. If it doesn't
rain in December, then
trust to God that it will in
February and March.
If nary a drop falls in March,
then you knows that disaster
is at hand. In the great
droughts of 1877 and 1915
the inhabitants of the sertão
left for the Amazon in search
of riches and rubber. In this
century, the cities of the
southeast have become home
to thousands of migrants.
Dramas of almost biblical
proportions for a people in
whose promised land only
clouds bring a miracle.

Monte Santo-BA ©R. Linsker

* Alberto Rangel.   185

The inhabitant of the sertão has become illuminated from watching the heavens so long. They are the most devout people in Brazil.

Offerings in Monte Santo-BA ©R. Linsker / Right page: Sertão do Maranhão ©R. Linsker; Iraquara-BA ©R. Linsker; Dona Toinha's kitchen, Santana do Cariri-CE ©R. Linsker

WATERS OF

WHAT HAVE WE DONE WITH OUR WATER? DESCENDANTS OF INDIANS THAT WE ARE, OUR LIVES WILL ALWAYS BE LINKED TO RIVERS. YOU ONLY HAVE TO ARRIVE IN ANY SMALL COMMUNITY IN BRAZIL WHERE THERE IS WATER. THERE'LL BE A BOY IN THE WATER. THERE'LL BE A WOMAN WASHING CLOTHES IN THE WATER, A FISHERMAN EARNING HIS LIVING FROM THE WATER. WATER IS DELIGHTFUL, BUT IT HAS ITS DARK SIDE: MOST DISEASES IN BRAZIL ARE TRANSMITTED THROUGH WATER. LACK OF BASIC SANITATION IN A LARGE PART OF THE COUNTRY AND THE ABSENCE OF PREVENTATIVE MEASURES WITH WATER DRAWN DIRECTLY FROM RIVERS FOR POPULAR CONSUMPTION IS STILL THE PRINCIPAL CAUSE OF INFANT MORTALITY, BACTERIAL INFECTION AND COUNTLESS OTHER DISEASES THAT COULD BE EASILY AVOIDED WITH SIMPLE MEASURES.

BRAZIL

Left page: Foz do Iguaçu N.P.-PR ©L. McIntyre / Rio Caraívas-BA ©R. Linsker

WHILE MUCH OF THE WORLD IS ALREADY BEGINNING TO SUFFER FROM LACK OF WATER, OR LACK OF PURE WATER, BRAZIL STILL FEELS BUFFERED FROM THE PROBLEM, SITTING AS IT DOES ON TOP OF PERHAPS 20% OF THE PLANET'S FRESHWATER. WE HAVE THE WORLD'S GREATEST WATER POTENTIAL. BUT WHAT DO WE DO WITH IT?
THE FACT IS THAT LARGE CITIES SUCH AS SÃO PAULO, BELO HORIZONTE AND RIO DE JANEIRO, AMONG OTHERS, MAKE OUR IMMENSE MISUSE OF WATER EVIDENT. RIVERS SUCH AS THE PINHEIROS AND THE TIETÊ HAVE BEEN TURNED IN A FEW SHORT DECADES INTO OPEN SEWERS. THE PAMPULHA LAKE IN BELO HORIZONTE NO LONGER SUPPLIES WATER TO THE CITY, SO POLLUTED HAS IT BECOME. IN FACT, WATER FOR HUMAN CONSUMPTION IN OUR LARGE CITIES HAS TO BE BROUGHT FROM EVER FARTHER AFIELD. HOW FAR WE CAN WE GO IN OUR CARE-LESS WASTE OF WATER?

WHO KILLED OUR RIVERS AND FORESTS? SÃO PAULO OF THE ATLANTIC RAINFOREST. CLOUDS HEAVY WITH RAIN BLOW IN FROM THE COAST, HIT THE ESCARPMENTS OF THE COASTAL RANGE, DROP THEIR LOADS AND GIVE RISE TO MYRIAD RIVERS AND WATERFALLS ALONG THE COASTAL SERRA DO MAR MOUNTAIN RANGE.
IN MID-19TH CENTURY ONE COULD STILL SPEAK OF DRIZZLY SÃO PAULO, WHERE WOMEN CONSTANTLY COVERED THEIR HEADS TO PROTECT THEMSELVES FROM THE DAMP. HOWEVER, THE COUNTRY'S LARGEST CITY GREW BY DESTROYING THAT VERY FOREST. WE NO LONGER ENJOY THE HUMIDITY OF THE TREES AND THE DRIZZLE. OUR RIVERS, STREAMS AND LAKES OF CRYSTAL-CLEAR WATER ARE TODAY PIPED UNDER THE ASPHALT JUNGLE, FILLED WITH A FILTHY LIQUID. IN ONE OF THE MOST PRIVILEGED STATES IN BRAZIL IN TERMS OF WATER RESOURCES, WE ARE GRADUALLY SUBSTITUTING OUR WATERFALLS AND STREAMS FOR TREATMENT PLANTS... WHERE THERE WAS ONCE ABUNDANT WATER, NOW, IN THE DRY MONTHS, WE SUFFER FROM SCARCITY.

OLD
MAN
CHICO.

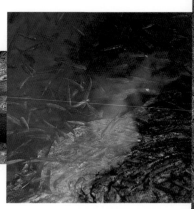

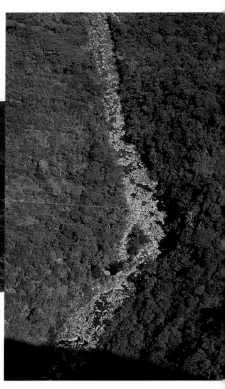

Source of the São Francisco, Serra da Canastra N.P.-MG ©R. Linsker; Casca D'Anta, Serra da CanastraN.P.-MG ©R. Linsker

IT IS THE LONGEST RIVER ENTIRELY WITHIN BRAZILIAN TERRITORY.

TIMIDLY SPRINGING TO LIFE FROM A SWAMP IN THE HIGHLANDS

OF THE CANASTRA MOUNTAIN RANGE, FOUR KILOMETERS LATER,

ALREADY WIDE AND SWIFT, IT PLUNGES ALMOST 200 METERS. THAT'S

ITS WAY OF DESCENDING THE MOUNTAINS, IN ONE ALMIGHTY

WATERFALL. AFTER CANASTRA, THE SÃO FRANCISCO TURNS NORTH
FOR 1,609 KM, UNTIL TURNING TO THE EAST FOR A FURTHER 277 KMS,
WHERE IT FINALLY FLOWS INTO THE ATLANTIC. NAVIGABLE BY MEDIUM
DRAUGHT BOATS FOR MOST OF ITS LENGTH, THE SÃO FRANCISCO
HAS BEEN CALLED THE RIVER THAT INTEGRATED A NATION.

Marajó-PA ©L. McIntyre; Parnaíba-PI ©R. Linsker

WATERS OF THE AMAZON. THE WATERS OF THE AMAZON AND THE TOCANTINS-ARAGUAIA RIVER SYSTEMS ALONE PROVIDE WATER TO 56% OF THE BRAZILIAN LANDMASS. THE RIVER AMAZON, CALLED BY ITS DISCOVERERS THE RIVER-SEA, HAS THE GREATEST VOLUME OF WATER IN THE WORLD, EMPTYING 100 THOUSAND CUBIC METERS OF WATER PER SECOND INTO THE ATLANTIC OCEAN, 20% OF THE WORLD'S FRESHWATER. IN THE AMAZON, THE RIVER BECOMES CONFUSED WITH LIFE ITSELF. HIGHWAY FOR CANOES AND BOATS, THE RIVER PROVIDES MANY WITH A LIVING, KEEPS HUNGER AT BAY, AND IS RESPONSIBLE FOR LEGENDS SUCH AS THAT OF THE RIVER PORPOISE WHO SEDUCES MAIDENS.

A BOY
    PLAYING IN WATER.

A PATCHWORK OF WATER. IN BRAZIL'S CENTRAL PLATEAU, IN THE MIDST OF THE CERRADO, THREE GREAT RIVER BASINS ARE BORN FLOWING IN DIFFERENT DIRECTIONS: THE RIVER SÃO FRANCISCO FLOWING NORTH-EAST, THE PARAGUAY-PARANA TOWARD THE SOUTHEAST AND THE TOCANTINS-ARAGUAIA TOWARD THE NORTH. THESE ARE THE SO-CALLED PATCHWORK WATERS, RESPONSIBLE FOR THE BIRTH OF IMMENSE RIVERS.

BRAZIL IS
A COUNTRY OF BOYS
PLAYING IN WATER.

Cachoeira-BA ©R. Linsker / Right page: Chapada Diamantina N.P.-BA ©R. Linsker

The city, a collective dream,
an urgent need for community.

BRASILCIDADE

photography and text: R. Linsker

The city where it is time that builds,
carves streets and avenues,
which gives form, transforms, and
Sometimes deforms the dream into
A nightmare.

The Brazilian city, a being in constant
mutation, something always unfinished
so that, incomplete, it never
stops ...dreaming.

BRASÍLIA

Courage
dreamed to make
Brazil take flight,
not as a plane,
but a bird.

MANAUS

Dreamed on the banks where the waters of the Rivers Solimões and Negro meet, perhaps not a dream but rather a delirium, where the Indian Amazon confronts the modernity coming upstream.

RIO DE JANEIRO

The planet's most beautiful and sensual geomor-
phology doesn't fit in its curves, a vertically and
horizontally sinuous city.

SALVADOR

Salvador adapted the dream to her cliffs, the upper town contrasting with the lower, and the Lacerda elevator lifting us to the future.

SÃO PAULO

São Paulo
industrialized
the dream,
"the power
of money,
that builds
and destroys
all things
beautiful".*

OFFERTORY

Photography: R. Linsker

OFFERTORY:

IT WAS A LITTLE HOUSE STANDING ALONE IN
THE MIDDLE OF THE SERTÃO. OF ABUNDANCE, JUST A FEW
PALM TREES THAT WERE ALREADY BEING CUT FOR THE CATTLE, IN THIS,
ONE OF THE WORST YEARS OF THE DROUGHT. TWO OR THREE STOOLS IN THE
LIVING ROOM, THE FRESH SMELL OF AN EARTHEN FLOOR. SHADE WITHIN AND A
BIT OF FRIENDLY CONVERSATION OFFERED LIKE A GIFT FOR US TRAVELERS WHO HAD
BEEN UNDER A SCALDING SUN FOR HOURS. AND THEN SWEET, WEAK COFFEE WAS
SERVED IN SMALL AGATE CUPS ALONG WITH A FEW BISCUITS. THIS WAS NO
DOUBT THE LAST DREGS OF COFFEE AND THE LAST REMAINING BISCUITS
ON THE KITCHEN SHELVES, GIVEN SO GENEROUSLY TO THE
STRANGERS. WE FOUND IT DIFFICULT
TO SWALLOW.

FIVE HUNDRED YEARS AGO, PERO VAZ DE CAMINHA INTUITED THAT EVERY SEED PLANTED IN BRAZIL WOULD MULTIPLY. THE BRAZILIAN EARTH IS GIVING, AND THE PEOPLE AS A WHOLE ARE THE HEIRS OF THIS GENEROSITY. THE GENEROSITY, FLEXIBILITY AND COMPASSION OF THE BRAZILIAN HAS ITS DRAWBACKS. EVEN EXECUTIONERS BENEFIT FROM OUR INFINITE PATIENCE. AND SO BRAZIL IS A VICTIM OF ITSELF.

IN 1994, SR. PEDRO DIAS DE AGUIAR UNDERTOOK A WELL-ORGANIZED, SPON-
SORED EXPEDITION AROUND BRAZIL, ALONG WITH HIS BROTHER AND A
TRUSTED RANCH HAND, MOUNTED ON HORSEBACK, WHICH LASTED FOR
TWO YEARS. THEY WERE TRAVELING IN TOCANTINS STATE AFTER MANY
MONTHS ON THE ROAD, WHEN ON CROSSING A RIVER THEY SPOTTED A
MAN FISHING. THEY STOPPED FOR INFORMATION, AS IT SEEMED THEY WERE
NOT FAR FROM THE RENDEZVOUS AGREED WITH THE BACK-UP TEAM. THEIR

Tucumã-PA; Banana-PA; Black beans-BA; Pepper-BA

DIRECTIONS CONFIRMED, THEY PREPARED TO MOVE ON, AFTER A QUICK EXCHANGE ON THE QUALITY OF THE FISHING, WHEN THE MAN INSISTED THEY TAKE A FISH WITH THEM TO EAT LATER ON. SR. PEDRO PROTESTED THAT IT WAS VERY KIND, BUT THEY DIDN'T WANT TO BE A BOTHER, ETC., BUT THE MAN INSISTED WITH MATHEMATICAL LOGIC: HE HAD TWO FISH, THEY HAD NONE. THE HORSEMEN REMEMBERED WELL THAT MANY A RICH MAN'S RANCH IN SÃO PAULO HAD CLOSED ITS GATES ON THEM.

Cashew fruit-PI; Herbs-CE; Pumpkin-BA; Dendê-BA

SALVE, SALVE!

(...) If we have to **pawn the essence** of our character

in order to be like the rest of the world,

I challenge you to answer me from the heart:

Beloved, adored motherland ...
Who is it that will save you now? Who will save you?

We always dream fervently that it is Brazil,

Keeping hope alive until the day we die.

For how much longer will that which is joyful, that which is pure,

Continue to shine resplendently?

A giant you will always be.

Will you continue handsome, strong and brave?

Your future is a reflection of our negligence today.

Adored land,

Out of thousands there is none to compare with thee,

Beloved motherland.

For us, children of this land, you were always a kind mother.

Forgive us, Brazil.

BRAZIL IS ONE OF THE WORLD'S LARGEST PRO-DUCERS OF FOOD AND YET ONE QUARTER OF THE COUNTRY'S PEOPLE SUFFER FROM HUNGER. THE COUNTRY WITH THE GREATEST AMOUNT OF FOREST IS ALSO THE GREATEST DESTROY-ER OF FORESTS: WE DESTROY 15,000 SQ. KM OF TREES PER YEAR IN THE AMAZON ALONE. THE WORLD'S FIFTH BIGGEST COUNTRY SQUEEZES 75% OF ITS POPULATION INTO CITIES. THIS EXODUS HAS NOT, HOWEVER, REDUCED THE PRESSURE ON NATURE. ONLY 7% OF THE ORIGINAL ATLANTIC RAINFOREST, THE MOST BRAZILIAN OF ECOSYSTEMS, REMAINS. THE CERRADO[1], FOR YEARS CON-SIDERED UGLY, TWISTED AND PARCHED, IS NOW FINALLY BEING SEEN AS POSSESSING A PRICELESS DIVERSITY OF VEGETATION, WITH ENORMOUS MEDICINAL POTENTIAL IN ITS PLANT LIFE. UNFORTUNATELY, WE ARE TOO LATE. THE CERRADO IS BEING TURNED INTO CHARCOAL OR TORN UP FOR PASTURE AND SOYBEANS. IN THE DRY SEASON, THE INTE-RIOR OF THE COUNTRY BURNS WHITE HOT. IT IS BURNED OVER TO CLEAR LAND FOR PAS-TURE, TO OPEN UP ROADS OR MERELY THROUGH CARELESSNESS.
DURING THESE MONTHS, THE NORMALLY AZURE SKIES TURN AN ASHEN GRAY. THE EYES WATER, PERHAPS FROM SADNESS.

1. Cerrado = scrub vegetation of the sertão

Picos-PI ©R. Linsker

SINCE THE DISCOVERY OF GOLD AND DIAMONDS IN THE COUNTRY'S INTERIOR IN THE MID-18TH CENTURY, BRAZIL HAS BEEN A MINERAL EXPORTING COUNTRY. MINERAL WEALTH IS THE RESULT OF THE COUNTRY'S ANCIENT AND DIVERSE GEOLOGICAL FORMATIONS. AS USUAL IN THE HISTORY OF BRAZIL, NEWS OF GOLD BRINGS HORDES OF MEN WITH LITTLE OR NOTHING TO THEIR NAMES, ILLITERATE, CARRIERS AND TRANSMITTERS OF CHRONIC DISEASE. FAR MORE LIKELY THAN BECOMING RICH, THE GOLD PROSPECTOR IS ALMOST CERTAIN TO SPREAD DISEASES SUCH AS MALARIA, FEVERS AND CHOLERA AMONG THE NATIVE POPULATIONS. RIVERS ARE POLLUTED WITH MERCURY RUN-OFF, CONTAMINATING THE FISH AND POISONING THE MEN AND WOMEN WHO LIVE OFF THEM.

A SIGNIFICANT PART OF OUR MINERAL RESERVES ARE LOCATED IN THE AMAZON REGION AND ON INDIGENOUS RESERVES. THE CHALLENGE IS TO PREVENT THE EXTRACTION OF MINERAL WEALTH FROM DESTROYING LOCAL PEOPLES AND THEIR WAY OF LIFE AS WELL AS THE DESTRUCTION OF OUR IMMENSE BIO-DIVERSITY.

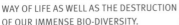

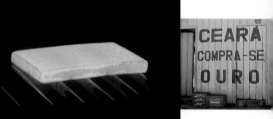

Congonhas ©Miguel Aun; Usiminas, Ipatinga ©Miguel Aun; São Gabriel da Cachoeira-AM ©R. Linsker   241

THE COUNTRY WAS BORN UNDER THE SIGN OF THE DEVASTATION OF ITS FORESTS: OUR FIRST EXPORT PRODUCT WAS A RED WOOD FROM WHICH A DEEP DYE WAS EXTRACTED. BRAZILWOOD GAVE ITS NAME TO THE COUNTRY, AND IN SO DOING GAVE ITS LIFE. FOR FIVE CENTURIES WE HAVE BEEN TAKING TIMBER, BURNING LAND, TILLING THE SOIL TO EXHAUSTION, MOVING ON TO DO THE SAME ELSEWHERE, AS IF THE COUNTRY WAS INFINITE AND THE FOREST WOULD NEVER END. THE WORLD'S LARGEST FOREST IN THE AMAZON HAS

ALREADY LOST 12% OF ITS ORIGINAL AREA. IT IS ESTIMATED THAT OUR IMMENSE BIO-DIVERSITY IS LOSING FROM 8,000 TO 28,000 SPECIES PER YEAR. PHOTOGRAPHER PEDRO MARTINELLI, WHO HAS DEDICATED THE BEST PART OF HIS LIFE TO LIFE IN THE AMAZON ASKS: "IN ONE HUNDRED YEARS, WHEN THE FOREST IS A DISTANT MEMORY, WILL WE BE REMEMBERED BY HISTORY AS THE GENERATION THAT HAD EVERYTHING – SATELLITES, GPS, PLANES WITH RADAR, TECHNOLOGY AND VARIOUS THEORIES – AND STILL DID NOTHING?"

What is public can never be private.
Child labor is not childhood.

THE END OF THE LINE: MISSING THE TRAIN OF HISTORY.
BRAZIL, A COUNTRY OF CONTINENTAL PROPORTIONS, HAS LET ITS RAILROAD
SYSTEM DECAY, GIVING PRIORITY TO HIGHWAY TRANSPORT. WHY?

BRAZIL DOESN'T KNOW WHAT IT IS LOSING. IN FACT, ONLY A VERY FEW DO KNOW. MOST PEOPLE TAKE CARE OF THEIR OWN BACKYARD, AS IF IT WERE THE EXTENT OF THEIR WORLD. THE NEIGHBORING STREET IS AS IF A FOREIGN LAND. AT THE HEART OF OUR HOUSE, IN THE MIDST OF OUR LIVES, THERE IS A TAP GIVING US WATER, BUT WE HAVE NO THIRST TO FIND OUT ANY FURTHER. BUT THE WATER WE DRINK COMES FROM THE MOUNTAINS, AND THE MOUNTAINS ARE BEING DEFORESTED AND INVADED BY ILLEGAL HOUSING SUBDIVISIONS. IN THE FUTURE, INSTEAD OF BEING ABLE TO DRINK PURE WATER, WILL WE BE ABLE TO DRINK THE FLUID OF THIS ILLEGAL ACTIVITY? DO YOU REALLY THINK SO? WE CAN ALREADY FEEL HOW MUCH THE CLIMATE HAS CHANGED IN RECENT DECADES AND HOW THE CITY HAS HEATED UP. BUT DOES ANYONE REMEMBER THAT WE USED TO LIVE IN THE MIDST OF THE ATLANTIC RAINFOREST AND THERE WERE TREES AND SHADE SURROUNDING OUR LIVES

Brazilian flora ©R. Linsker

AND THAT THEIR ABSENCE MAKES A HUGE DIFFERENCE? AND WHEN PEOPLE VOICE

THEIR WORRIES OVER WHAT COULD HAPPEN IN THE AMAZON, THE RESPONSE IS OFTEN:

"AH... BUT IT'S SO FAR AWAY..." WHEN THEY FELL THE LAST TREE OF A SPECIES THAT

HIDES AN INGREDIENT THAT COULD SAVE OUR LIVES, ITS ABSENCE WILL BE FELT MUCH

CLOSER. BRAZIL IS NOT EVEN AWARE THAT IT IS LOSING THE MOST BEAUTIFUL THINGS IN

THE WORLD: HOMEMADE FISHING CANOES GLIDING TO AND FRO ACROSS THE SEA,

DESERTED BEACHES, NOISY FLOCKS OF MACAWS AND SO MANY OTHER ANIMALS,

BARREL ORGANS IN THE CITY, MEDICINAL PLANTS IN THE CERRADO, THE ESTHETIC OF

THE COUNTRYSIDE, THE TREES OF THE AMAZON, RIVERS IN WHICH TO FISH AND SWIM,

PILGRIMAGES AND RELIGIOUS FESTIVALS, THE CHILDHOOD OF HUNDREDS OF THOU-

SANDS OF CHILDREN. IN THE FUTURE, PROGRESS WILL NOT BE SUFFICIENT TO SATISFY

OUR NOSTALGIA. THE WORST KIND OF BLIND MAN IS HE WHO WISHES NO ONE ELSE TO SEE.

IN 1945 THREE BROTHERS, CLÁUDIO, ORLANDO AND LEONARDO VILLAS-BÔAS, THOUGHT THAT PROGRESS WAS ARID AND INSIPID AND LEFT FOR THE FORESTS

AND RIVERS OF CENTRAL BRAZIL. IF ANYONE REALLY DISCOVERED BRAZIL, IT WAS THESE MEN. THEY SAW SUCH

RICHNESS IN OUR ORIGINAL WAY OF LIVING THAT THEY DEDICATED THEIR LIVES TO THE INDIAN CAUSE AND THE CREATION OF A VAST NATURAL RESER

VATION, THE INDIGENOUS PARK OF THE XINGU. AH... IF ONLY BRAZIL HAD MORE ORLANDOS, CLÁUDIOS AND LEONARDOS...